CW01095477

COWBRIDGE AND DISTRICT
REMEMBERED
1900 – 1950

COWBRIDGE AND DISTRICT REMEMBERED 1900 - 1950

Memories of life in Aberthin, Cowbridge, Llanblethian, Llysworney, Maendy, Trerhyngyll and Ystradowen in the early years of the twentieth century

COWBRIDGE RECORD SOCIETY
2002

Published by
Cowbridge Record Society
1 Mill Park, Cowbridge, CF71 7BG

Produced by
Keith Brown & Sons Ltd
55 Eastgate, Cowbridge

© Cowbridge Record Society 2002

ISBN 0 9537029 3 6

PREFACE

The idea for this book came after reading two very interesting reminiscences about life in the area, written by Bert Jenkins and by the late Ralph Bird. Both had been written mainly for the benefit of family members, but I felt that they could well be enjoyed by a wider audience. Our thanks are due to Bert Jenkins and to the family of Ralph Bird for their permission to include large extracts from their work, and also to the eleven other contributors who have so willingly told us of their memories of life in our area in the first half of the twentieth century. Without them, there would have been no book! Nearly all the photographs, too, come from the contributors; in addition, we thank Danny Radcliffe and Mary Wallis for their help. Together the memoirs and the photos provide a vivid picture of life in the town and district from 1900 to 1950.

Thanks are also due to those who helped in recording the contributions - Betty Alden, Deborah Fisher and Don Gerrard, to Keith Jones for his proofreading, to José Rawlins for the cover design, and to Hilary Thomas and Brian James for their expert guidance.

We also thank Keith and Eurion Brown for their printing expertise, and for producing yet another book which is pleasing to handle and to read.

Jeff Alden
Editor

CONTENTS

RALPH BIRD, COWBRIDGE

Ralph Bird, 1897-1987, wrote down his reminiscences, mainly for his own family, in about 1980. He was the founder of RS Bird Ltd and was instrumental in developing the grass-cutting side of the business which is still run by the Bird family today. These extracts deal with Cowbridge in the first two decades of the twentieth century, but the photo shows Ralph with Percy Thrower in the garden centre in the 1970s.

I was born in 1897, so my earliest memories are of the beginning of the twentieth century, but I have some knowledge of family events before that. My uncle Nathaniel was in charge of the family ironmongery business in the 1880s. He was a great character and highly respected throughout the neighbourhood. Before he died aged sixty-six in 1893 he started a fund to build an institute in the town; his contribution virtually covered the cost of the building, which is at the rear of the Town Hall. When he died, my father who was an engineer and surveyor by profession took over the business. As Borough Surveyor, he lived first at Brynhyfryd and then at St Quentin's, both large houses in Llanblethian. At that stage in his life, he had in his employ a coachman-gardener and two housemaids.

Father, as the local surveyor, caused all the refuse from the area to be tipped in Waun-y-Gaer (the site of the garden centre) because it was so low-lying that every winter it became completely flooded. The water often came right up to the stables which were at the bottom of the garden. The High Street near the Town Hall also became flooded and sometimes the water could not be kept out of the shop and the house. The dumping of the refuse largely cured the trouble in the field, but not completely so until the County Council straightened out the course of the river and dredged the bed deeply. The line of beautiful willow trees in what is now the garden centre was planted by my father during that period.

Our garden, with two lawns, flower beds and borders and a large bush of pampas grass, was at the rear of the house (14 High Street, where Martin's is today). It contained a large lean-to greenhouse which housed an extensive vine, which originated from a cutting taken from Hampton Court. Behind the garden were stables and beyond the stables was the meadow of Waun-y-Gaer.

There used to be quite a long lean-to shed extending from our stables towards the church. The first part of this shed was used as a blacksmith's shop, worked by Harry Webb whose wife subsequently ran a small grocery business where the Ogmore Vale bakery now operates. Harry was a great character and would allow the children to operate the bellows. There were actually two bellows - one either side of the forge. His assistant was Gwyn Thomas, a stocky man who could strike resounding blows with his hammer.

Harry Webb eventually moved to a new smithy at the rear of Arthur John's premises in Bear Lane, and he was joined by Gilead Spencer who was a wheelwright and carriage builder. The smith and the wheelwright

RS Bird & Co at 14 High Street, Cowbridge, 1920s

were complementary to each other. When the smithy was at Waun-y-Gaer there was an understanding between Dad and Harry that horses could be housed in our stables when our own pony was not in residence.

Running alongside the stable of the Butchers Arms (10 High Street) was a very large wooden shed which belonged to Dr Meller. In it he kept all sorts of gardening requisites, including large quantities of canes - some of which were purloined by me for the window games, which you shall read about later. The doctor had a large garden at the rear of his house and a still larger one down the Town Mill road. This was bounded on the south side by the drive leading to the Verlands where Mr Tom John lived. I must have spent scores of hours assisting the doctor in his gardens. He swept the board at whatever flower show he chose to exhibit.

Our shop was kept open during the week until 6.00pm, and until 9.00pm on Saturdays, or even later if there was a customer to be served. Every day a wide assortment of hardware was put on display on the pavement. Above what is now the covered right of way to the west of the shop was a small warehouse, and such items as rolls of wire netting were lifted from the pavement by means of a hand-operated hoist, the arm of which swung out over the pavement. At that time there was no objection to cluttering up the pavement. The passageway was also used as a place of storage and a little way down was a fifty-gallon tank of paraffin. This sold at about 4d per gallon. The courtyard was stone flagged and every Saturday morning it was the custom to use hard brooms and sand and water to clean the surface. My part in the proceedings was to go to buy a bucket of sand for the price of one halfpenny from Mr Trott at the Lodging House, the large house at the junction of the Bear Lane and Eagle Lane. (There were many tramps in those days and some of them got a ticket from the police station which entitled them to a night's lodging).

★★★

At that time the house and shop were lit by acetylene gas and we had an acetylene generator in the courtyard adjoining the house. We developed a fair trade in carbide among the large country houses which used the same means of lighting. The carbide was packed in round one-hundredweight drums and was not easy to handle. It was often my job to re-charge the generator, which was really a miniature gas works. Sometimes the smell of the half-consumed wet carbide was pretty bad. All deliveries from the shop at that time were made by means of a horse-drawn dray. The odd motor car now began to appear - a Daimler at Penllyn Castle whose registration number was L6, a chain-driven Wolseley belonging to Sir Thomas Mansel Franklen of St Hilary, L9, another Wolseley and a Talbot belonging to Mr EH Ebsworth at Llandough Castle and a White steam car which Sir Francis Price Fothergill used at Hensol Castle. Mr PT Bassett, a veterinary surgeon whose home was at New Beaupre, and whose brother lived at Crossways, used a Humber three-wheeler with tiller steering to visit his sick animals. The local registration numbers were L for Glamorgan, BO for Cardiff, DW for Newport and CY for Swansea.

The early years of motoring were a frightening time for horses, and when going to Llandough Castle we would stop at Lake Farm and listen very intently in the hope that we would catch the sound of any motor car that might be coming from the castle. It was always our practice when on country roads to be looking out for clouds of dust which told us a car was somewhere ahead.

The general condition of roads was pretty bad. Pot holes abounded and a heavy layer of dust was always in evidence. In those days roads were repaired in a very primitive way, although there were steam rollers in use. These were adorned with the emblem of a rampant horse in brass which was very impressive. It was quite appropriate too, because few horses could be persuaded to pass them. A large heap of stones would be carted to the side of the road and stone breakers were employed to break the stones up by means of special hammers. The stone breakers wore spectacles fitted with very fine mesh wire gauzes to prevent splinters from entering the eye. The broken stones had to pass through a large sieve and those which did not get through had to be cracked again. It was an onerous job during bad weather and it was the duty of the surveyor to check the work every few days. I often went with Dad on these journeys which were made in a horse-drawn gig.

In the main street the road was tarred and I vaguely remember Dad being sued as the responsible officer of the local Council by Colonel Watson of Llansannor Court. He had many valuable horses and one of them slipped on the tar before it had been sanded, and sustained serious injury. There was great relief when the charge of carelessness was dismissed by the court.

If anyone was gravely ill in a house bordering the main street, it was the custom to lay down much sand and some straw in the immediate neighbourhood to deaden the noise made by the horse-drawn vehicles. There were of course many of these. Brakes drawn by two, three or four horses used to pull up on Saturdays and Sundays at some of the Cowbridge public houses. When ascending the Tumble or any similar hill a number of the passengers were expected to get out and walk.

★★★

In the building now occupied by the electrical shop at the side of the Town Hall there was a bakehouse operated by a Mr Gibbs. He used to spend a great deal of his time during the winter afternoons fast asleep by the fire in the Institute reading room. This room was on the left of the entrance hall and it contained most of the daily newspapers, together with copies of *Punch*, the *Illustrated London News*, the *Tatler* and the *Sketch*. The *Strand* magazine was also available and this was very popular because each month it featured a Sherlock Holmes detective story. The periodicals were auctioned every year at Christmas time and each copy was collected by the successful bidder when the new edition was placed on the table. On the right of the hall was a similar room which acted as a library. The books were housed in glass cases which were kept locked, but opened every Monday evening. At the rear were two fairly large rooms, one for meetings whilst the other housed a large and a small billiards table. The caretaker was Mr Fred Knapton who lived in one of the three cottages to the right of the Institute and which were demolished in the 1930s.

The Armoury which was situated between the Blue Bell Inn and Mr Miles's grocery shop had an open forecourt (now the Filco car park) where we played lots of cricket. The wall nearest the Blue Bell was partially covered with ivy and had a small ledge about ten feet above the ground. If the cricket ball, after being hit, got lodged in the ivy, the fielders kept their places until Mr Miles was free to examine the position. It was he who decided whether a fielder would have caught the ball if it had not been trapped in the ivy; if he said yes, the batsman was given out.

Another childhood game was 'buttons': the game was to lean on the pavement by the gutter and throw the button along the floor to the wall of the house, the nearest being the winner who would win all the buttons in that particular throw. We also played tops and, of course, every autumn saw the emergence of our iron hoops; the girls used wooden ones. One game was to let the hoop go at full tilt down a slope, hit a large stone that had been placed in its path and then see the hoop leap into the air and jump over an obstacle. This often happened in the Slade Field opposite the old railway station and sometimes the hoop would clear the wooden railings and land on the road. If a hoop got fractured it was repaired for a penny or two by Harry Webb the blacksmith. A halfpenny at that time was a real coin of the realm. With it one could buy two and a half Woodbine, Cinderella or Ogden's Tabs cigarettes from Miss Stibbs, and the choice of sweets costing a halfpenny was quite extensive.

The Royal Oak Inn was run by the Fitzgerald family and, as Billy Fitzgerald was of our age, we were allowed sometimes to play in the skittle alley, the only one in the locality. We also did a bit of boxing in the skittle alley as Billy possessed two pairs of boxing gloves. The Horse and Groom and the Druid Hotel each had billiard tables.

***

In 1908 I became a day boy at Cowbridge Grammar School which was always known locally as the College. I still remember very vividly walking down Church Street on my first morning and I was very proud of the red cockerel on my black cap. It cost my parents £3 per term to keep me there. This represented a real sacrifice, because if one takes the cost of labour as a common denominator that £3 equalled about £70 in 1980, perhaps more. At that time wages for non-skilled workers were in the region of £1.10s to £2. I was at the school for six years; my headmaster was the Revd William Franklen Evans, and the assistant masters were David Percival Jones, Charles Mayo, RC Hadland, Ralph Jones and Ronald St Clair Wall. Of these, Ronald Wall (who was a former pupil) and Charles Mayo were killed in the First World War.

Cricket was played in the summer term, soccer in the winter term and during the first half of Easter term, whilst hockey took up the second half. Every Friday morning we had drill or PT or were taken for a long walk. Sergeant Bradbury was our tutor and he was a very decent chap. He lived next door to the Wesleyan chapel. We also had a miniature shooting range and I still have a medal I won in 1909. On Sundays the boys (including myself) wore Eton jackets and striped trousers. The jackets were cut very short and were known as bum-freezers.

The Fifth form usually had a dozen boys, the Fourth and the Modern form each about ten, whilst the Third form was always the largest with eighteen or twenty pupils. There was no Form II and the First form usually had less than a dozen. The ratio of pupils to tutors ensured that each boy had a fair share of personal attention. There were only about fifty or sixty pupils before the war and most were boarders. Some of the boarders came from homes which were distant from Cowbridge, such as the brothers Deza from Brazil. There were only two in the Sixth form in 1908; they were Jones *major* (Boggy) and Davies *major* (Plug). Jones *major* married a daughter of Mr AS Evans and was later knighted for services as a government official in west Africa.

In the summer, school hours were from 6.55 to 8.00, 8.55 to 12 noon, 1.55 to 4.00 and 6.55 to 8.20. In the winter the early morning sessions started at 7.30 instead of 6.55. Wednesday and Saturday afternoons were free, but we were in trouble if we did not turn up for games on the school field. I think my happiest hours were those spent at the cricket games we played alongside Dr Shepherd's hedge which formed the boundary of the garden belonging to Dynevor Cottage. There was a large garden where the Old Hall car park now stands and, if we could possibly clear the garden wall with a big hit, we scaled the wall and never found the ball until we had sampled the lovely peaches which grew all along the south wall adjoining Old Hall grounds.

I used to play in goal for the school both at soccer and hockey and played for several years in the cricket First XI. I enjoyed cricket most of all. I was reasonably successful at the school sports, winning several prizes.

I wouldn't say my behaviour was better than average and I often got the stick. This could be terribly painful as administered by WFE. Most fun we had in the evening studies when we got armed with strong elastic which propelled a really hard piece of compressed paper held V-shape by the teeth. Our targets were usually those who 'swotted' too much but this form of target practice was much disliked by the master in charge and often resulted in the culprit being sent to the Headmaster's study for the stick. In the early days, there was a very elite girls' school run by a Miss Culverwell at what is now Great House. My sister was a pupil there and it became known that one or two of the boarders used to make a precarious escape from the dormitory at night time to meet the girls in the churchyard.

★★★

During the school holidays we used to do some stupid things, usually in the dark. One night we got a hiding from the landlord of the Masons Arms because we were in the Market and had securely fixed a pin into the frame of the window to the right of the side door. To the pin was attached strong cotton and a few inches from the pin a large button was fixed to the cotton. The cotton reached over the market wall. Every time we jerked it the button rapped the window pane. Out would come the landlord and of course there was no-one to be seen. On the third or fourth occasion he must have spotted the button, so he went down his garden and came upon us from the rear. He laid into us good and proper! This game was called 'tap tap'.

On another occasion we attached the black cotton to the knocker of Mr John David's door. He lived at Llwyncelyn and was the founder of the firm of John David, Watts and Morgan, auctioneers and estate agents. We trailed cotton across the road and crouched behind the railings of Old Hall opposite. The knocker would knock, the door duly opened, no-one to be seen. Perhaps it was the second knock that prompted Mr. David to stay inside the door and as soon as it knocked again he flung the door open. This time the cotton broke and we all ran off hell for leather. In those days there was very little traffic after dark; our greatest risk was the possibility of a pedestrian walking into the cotton.

The worst thing we did was to demolish the contents of Miss Stibbs's right-hand window. This is where the Ogmore Vale bakery shop now operates. At the base of the window there were round holes presumably for ventilation. We would stare into the window and push a garden cane through the hole. One night the background to the window display consisted of 5lb bags of flour mounted one on top of the other. By pushing the bottom ones with the cane the whole lot would collapse. We did this sort of thing fairly often, but Miss Stibbs was very old and it was rather unkind to play her up in this way.

In Mr Bill Pickard's grocery shop in Eastgate, the side of the rectangular window was boarded up but not very tidily. Through gaps in the boards we could push in our magic wand and lay low the cardboard boxes, the show cards and anything else he had in the window.

★★★

In the three garages which were operating in Cowbridge at that time, car hiring was very popular. Mr Arthur Evans at the Armoury ran a Charron limousine and a Humber Tourer. Mr Mills of the High Street Garage ran Model T Fords whilst Mr Jones (West End Garage) first had an 18hp V twin Riley and then in 1912 he went to Scotland to take delivery of a 12hp Argyll. This was a lovely open four-seater with torpedo body and was the first make of motor car to be fitted with front wheel brakes. The twin-cylinder Riley was most difficult to start when cold. All of these cars were started by handle. In the winter it was often necessary to jack up one rear wheel of the Model T Ford to ease the friction in the transmission before the engine could be started. There was of course always a chance of the car jumping off the jack when the engine did start and the rear wheels began to revolve. In such a case the chap at the handle had to be pretty quick off the mark!

But the fun really was with the motor bikes. Mr Evans had the Triumph, Humber and the Royal Enfield; Mr Mills had the Premier, the

James and later the Rover and the Lincoln Elk; Mr Jones had the BSA and the Rudge Multi. Hill climbs and reliability trials were very popular and many are the tales connected with them. Billy Jones imported a semi-professional rider called Clisset from Barry to compete at the Ewenny Hill climb and this caused quite a sensation. Races from the Town Hall to the top of Primrose Hill were frequent events, scouts being placed at the junction of the Aberthin and Llanblethian roads to stop all traffic.

The Brewery Office opposite the Duke was manned by Mr Joe Staien who lived at St Hilary. He had a James motorbike and a very popular type of coach-built sidecar called the Canoelet which cost 12 guineas. It was possible to buy a wicker sidecar for as little as £3.15s.0d. Every time Joe went home to lunch he would run alongside the bike and as soon as he had gained a little momentum (going downhill) he would drop the exhaust lever, start the engine, get on the bike and before he had passed the Town Hall he would have transferred himself to the sidecar. At that time there were no clutches or gear boxes on motor bikes. It was direct drive by belt from the engine pulley to the belt drum on the rear wheel. Joe would get up a good speed, blowing his bulb horn nearly all the time and would shoot past the crossroads where the lights now are at a good 30-35mph so that he could climb Primrose Hill. He never had an accident.

At a later date Dr Temple, who was an assistant to Dr Meller and lived at Llantwit Major, went one better. He had a 6hp Royal Enfield and sidecar in which he always sat whilst on his rounds. He had the footbrake pedal extended through into the sidecar for emergency stops and he also had a huge klaxon horn which could be heard for hundreds of yards. The clutch was within comfortable reach and this was, of course, a great advantage to the driver in the sidecar.

Bill Croome, the sweep, had a Premier and he carried all his brushes and canes in his sidecar. George Durston the butcher also had a Premier and sidecar for delivering meat. George was also a part-time AA patrolman and used to spend his Sundays directing traffic at the point where the Porthcawl road leaves the A48.

On fine Sundays a few motor cyclists, usually from Cardiff, would frequently come to Cowbridge and stop outside one of the pubs. They were much admired by the locals - there were beautiful Red Indians, Harley Davidsons, a four-cylinder Henderson and sometimes a lovely water-cooled Scott which had a twin-cylinder two-stroke engine and was of unconventional design.

★★★

Although I played association football for Cowbridge, my great love was cricket, and during the summer my brother Bruce and I played most Wednesday and Saturday afternoons. Cowbridge had a very fine ground and always employed a professional. A vivid recollection is that of a wreath in the shape of a cricket bat which the Cowbridge Cricket Club placed on the grave of Mr Russell the professional, who was probably the greatest batsman ever to play for Cowbridge. He made many centuries and more than one double century. Other 'pros' included Trevor Preece, Gange (who played for Gloucestershire and was a fast bowler), Geary, Pell and Edwards. The first war meant the loss of three of the five Dunn brothers, all of whom were fine cricketers. The Revd Owen Jones (known as Bingo) was quite a character with his slow leg breaks, unorthodox cricket apparel and some original strokes while at the wicket!

Croquet was played immediately inside the entrance gates to the cricket field and the box containing the equipment was kept at Stafford House, then occupied by Mr WA James, the builder. I was always delighted to have a game of croquet. Before the war a bowling green was constructed near the north corner of the ground, not far from the further rugby posts as they now stand. It was however built by amateurs, and the sport never became really popular before it was abandoned.

Cowbridge had a very good soccer side which played on the far side of the cricket field; Dick Moynan, who was a trainee surgeon, always played his soccer wearing white gloves. There was also a good rugby XV which played on a field at the back of Cae Stumpie immediately opposite Heath House garden. The stumpy field (as it was known) also used to stage live pigeon shoots. Each bird was placed in a collapsible box which was opened by means of a long length of cord – a cruel sport.

★★★

My mother was a staunch member of Ramoth Baptist church. We were not allowed to have a Sunday newspaper, whilst cycling on the Sabbath was sternly forbidden. The family had to attend Ramoth twice each Sunday, plus Sunday school in the afternoon, as well as the Band of Hope and a prayer meeting during the week. The Band of Hope was a weekly meeting for the youngsters at which volunteers sang or recited. It was good fun but I remember being much ridiculed by Bruce because on one occasion I decided that I would sing 'Somewhere the Sun is Shining' and, as I have no singing voice, I expect the entertainment must have been very laughable.

Sometimes we had a get-together around Christmas time in the school room where we had children's games. One that was quite exciting was to spin a tray in the centre of the room and call upon the sweetheart of the moment to catch it before it stopped spinning. Another great adventure was provided by the figure of a large donkey which had no tail. The detached tail had adhesive material at the top. Each competitor was blindfolded and tried to stick the tail on the donkey. The one nearest to the correct position was the prize winner.

Between seventy and eighty children went to Sunday school, and they were supposed to have a minimum attendance record to be eligible to join in the Sunday school treat. The most popular destination was Barry Island because of the lovely sands and the children's swimming pool. We believed that the tunnel through which the train passed was specially constructed to form part of the fun. Donkey rides were of course very popular. Sometimes we went by brake to the Leys, or to Marcross. The lighthouse and fog horn there were great attractions.

For several years in the early 1900s we enjoyed the entertainment provided by the Cowbridge Minstrels. They were like our present-day Black and White Minstrels - their faces and hands completely blacked up and their costumes were very good indeed. (Charles Davies the hairdresser was responsible for the make-up). They held concerts in the Town Hall, two each winter, singing popular comic songs and always producing a number of topical jokes. I still recall two of their jokes. 'Tell me, Sambo, if Queen Alexandra kissed King Edward and King Edward kissed Queen Alexandra, what public building would they represent?' Blank faces. 'Why - the Royal Exchange of course'. Enormous laughter. JW Hall was a hay merchant who lived at Rhoscelyn, hence the following: 'Say, Sambo, why is a load of hay like a piece of silver?' More blank faces. 'Because it is Hall marked, of course'.

★★★

There were three doctors in Cowbridge and they were looked upon with great respect. Dr Charles Booth Meller lived at Caercady House, a lovely house opposite the Bear Hotel. Dr Meller was an eccentric who never charged poor people for attendance and medicine, neither did he make any charge to any minister or clergyman. He always wore formal dress, a silk hat and frock coat. His mode of transport was by gig and stallion, accompanied always by his groom. He had several stallions, and the stables were located where the High Street Garage now stands, next door to Barclays Bank. Dr Meller was very fond of the Bird family and took good care of us. If I were ill he would bring me lots of oranges, and on many occasions he would present us with a crateful.

The other two doctors were Irish - Dr Hastings Torney who lived at Sorrento House and Dr Richard Moynan who lived at Woodstock House. Moynan was a good cricketer but he disliked fielding. He had an extraordinary understanding with his maidservant who, wearing a white apron with ribbons flying from her bonnet, would come across to the Bear Field hedge and then wave to the doctor. This, however, never occurred before the doctor had had his innings. The news was always the same, 'Sick patient getting worse, immediate attention needed', and off the doctor would go. Dr Moynan had a 10hp four-cylinder blue Humber two-seater which was looked after by Sgt Bill Brown, who was the Town Hall caretaker and driver of the fire engine. Dr Torney had a single-cylinder 6hp green De Dion two-seater.

In the garage run by Mr Mills there appeared in 1915 what in those days was considered to be a very desirable two-seater motor car. It was called an Enfield Autolette and we decided to buy it, for a very small sum, and I remember very vividly driving it out of the garage and down to 14 High Street. That short journey was a great adventure because I kept on going from one side of the road to the other. The road must have been perfectly clear, otherwise there would have been a collision.

Dr Meller, as I have said, had his stallions, but about the time we acquired the Enfield Autolette he, for some reason which I do not recall, gave up the horses and he asked Dena, my sister, if she would drive him around in the Enfield. Of course Dena was delighted and a charge per mile was agreed upon.

Now the Enfield was no ordinary motor car. In the first place it had a vertical twin-cylinder water-cooled engine and it was quite impossible to imagine the vibration which was set up at certain engine speeds. Perhaps between 24 and 27mph you would be shaken to pieces, but at 28mph it was very much better. The alleged rating was 8/9hp and this was insufficient to climb the Lake Hill with the doctor as passenger because he was really a very large man and must have weighed at least sixteen stone. When this was first discovered I believe I was driving as I remember reversing down the portion we had climbed and then turning into the road leading to Llandough. There we turned round and negotiated the hill in reverse gear, which had a very much lower ratio than the first forward gear. To be ascending the Lake Hill backwards was quite an experience but it was either that or go by some other route.

★★★

It must have been soon after the war started that I joined the Metropolitan Bank of England and Wales. I started at Pontypridd but after a year or so I was transferred to Cowbridge. The Cowbridge branch was where HRThomas now have their offices. It then became the London Joint City and Midland Bank and then the Midland Bank. The manager was Mr Robert Thomas, one of four farming brothers.

In those days the last post out from Cowbridge was at 8.20pm and there were occasions when I only just succeeded in catching it. The manager's interest in his Kerry sheep, which he kept at St Hilary, in his bees and in the building at that time of the Baptist manse were some of the reasons why I was kept late. As I was the junior clerk, it was my duty to copy letters after they were signed, place them in the envelopes, stamp the envelopes, place them in a special leather post bag and then post them at the post office. The leather bag was taken back to the bank on the following morning. The copying of letters was not done by means of carbon sheets, but by means of damp cloths. This process is probably worth relating. A special book with numbered, wafer-thin pages was kept to preserve a copy of every letter sent out. A damp cloth of special texture was placed above each page with the letter underneath and the book then placed in a press. Now this was very much a hit-or-miss method because success or failure depended upon many things. The cloth must not be too damp or too dry, the press must not be pressed too much or too little and the time the book stayed in the press was also very important.

If any one of the foregoing rules for letter copying was broken it could mean either a very faint and almost illegible copy being produced or else a copy which, although legible, meant that the actual letter to be posted could be a shambles. The ink could run from every word just as if flies had walked across it. Perhaps the worst to suffer was the manager's ink-written signature. I got into diabolical trouble many times because of this copying business and gradually became more and more frustrated with my job. Although I was classified by head office as being 'indispensable' I did not report for duty one morning, but instead went to the recruiting office in Cardiff and joined up as a despatch rider in the Motor Transport section of the RASC.

★★★

When I returned to Cowbridge after being discharged from the army, the business was at a low ebb because manufactured goods were very scarce indeed and we had lost the Lister engine agency to Arthur John. We did manage, I remember, to obtain a small supply of BSA 12-bore double-barrel hammerless shotguns with left hand choke which sold at the amazingly low price of 12 guineas. I became the proud possessor of one, and for many years enjoyed shooting, chiefly over the Flemingston moors after wildfowl.

We also bought a new Model T one-ton chassis with cab, upon which Gilead Spencer the wheelwright built a drop-side body and he also made wooden hoops upon which a brown canvas top was mounted, just like the old covered wagons.

In May 1922 on a lovely early summer morning, a telephone call which I happened to answer was destined to alter our whole way of life. It was from Mr Sydney Byass at Llandough Castle, asking whether we could arrange for him a demonstration at Llandough of one of the new Atco motor mowers. We arranged for the Atco demonstrator to come from Newport, and we stayed at the castle for some hours making quite sure that the gardener and the chauffeur were completely familiar with the operation and maintenance of the machine. I used the machine myself and thoroughly enjoyed doing so because it was very easy to handle. Having a nine-bladed cylinder, it cut beautifully. The sale of this first motor lawn mower was so exciting and inspiring that I made up my mind that mowers would provide us with a living.

That, of course, is another story.

GWYNETH WILLIAMS, COWBRIDGE

Mrs Williams, née Evans, was born in Cowbridge in 1907 and grew up here, living for most of her childhood in Eastfield House. After some time in England she has now returned to the town of her birth. These reminiscences mainly cover the period before 1925.

My grandfather was Samuel David Evans. His family owned weaving mills in Newcastle Emlyn in west Wales, and he moved to Cowbridge to open a drapery business. The shop and house where I was born was in the High Street. If you go down High Street, after Sloper's Alley (Verity's Court), there was Miss Griffiths's shop, then a small ironmonger's shop which was John's, then a house called Ty Hen, to which Thomas, the owner of the Bear, retired. Next to that was the shop which my grandfather started. He had a very large shop, covering 37 and 39 High Street, and which contained a gentlemen's outfitters, a shoe shop and a ladies' fashion shop. Among the tailors were Mr Marks, the church organist, and 'Coity' Williams, the manager. The shoe shop was managed by a man called Sid Knapton, from an old Cowbridge family. In those days, assistants lived in. The building had three floors, and on the top floor were workrooms where the seamsters used to do their work and where a few of the assistants lived. On the second floor were the bedrooms, and the rest of the house was on the ground floor, behind the shops. Many of the maids and servants came from Cardigan, and married local Cowbridge people. One married William David the butcher, and another married Frank Sanders, who looked after a smallholding in fields north of Bear Lane.

When my grandfather retired and moved to Barry, my father, Arthur Stephen Evans, took over the business. I was born in 1907 in our house behind the shop. I remember it was a very large house, with a billiard room.

When the motor business started, my father was very keen on it, and opened a garage next door to Miles the grocers (at what is today the entrance to the Filco car park). He sold two of the drapery shops, only keeping the gentlemen's tailors, and his younger brother, Fred Evans, took that over. We moved when I was very young to Eastfield House, when my father started the garage. He later built the big garage across the river. Here there had been three dilapidated cottages, and a shop, up some steps, which became Tucker's shop. These all had to be removed to build the garage.

My mother was one of the Johns of the Pentre brewery in the Rhondda, and my grandparents on that side originated from Llanharan. My grandfather, who started the brewery, lived in Caercady, near Welsh St Donats. He died after a hunting accident. One of my uncles farmed Marlborough Grange, while my uncle Tom John lived in the Verlands, and married Molly Llewellyn from Heath House; he later moved to the Armoury, and died there. My parents also lived in the Armoury for some time, and one of my sisters, Muriel - who was ten years older than I - was born there. She married William Jones, who was knighted for his work with the colonial service in the Gold Coast. When she was returning from Africa during the First World War for the birth of her first child, her ship was torpedoed off the coast of Ireland. She survived, luckily, and her son was born the following month.

On my father's side, I had three uncles - Samuel David Evans junior, Frederick, and Thomas Edward. Samuel was a solicitor, and lived at Glendare House (71 High Street); Fred, who ran the drapery, lived in Bridge House, (and his son, Dick, who was in the Royal Flying Corps, ran a garage in Llantwit Major after the war); Thomas became a rector in Chester.

I started my education at a kindergarten run by the two Miss Morrises of Great House, Llanblethian, in a room of Sanders's house at Town Mill. I went there with Margaret Jenkins and Carol Hopkins (the daughter of John Hopkins the monumental mason), but we soon went on to Miss Culverwell's school in Great House, next door down from 'Billy Pills', Thomas the chemist. They used to have to carry me across the road to school, because I hated going to school. There were boarders there, too, as it was quite a biggish school, but I lived at home. Next I was sent away to school in Richmond, but I came home almost immediately, and then went to 'the intermediate' - the High School.

March Fair, Cowbridge, about 1910

When I was a child, one of the highlights of the year was March Fair day about March 21st, when all the pubs were celebrating, and gypsies always came with their horses and you would see them parading the horses up and down the streets; they used to camp around Cowbridge then. The open market was held in the street outside Woodstock House and the Eagle, with small stalls. Studt's fair was the only 'joy fair', with roundabouts and so on - that was held in the Bear Field. There were terrific carnival celebrations at the end of the First World War.

I can also remember going on family outings by railway to Aberthaw, with picnic baskets, and then walking all the way to Fontygary, spending the day there and then walking back to the station. Freda Mills (of the Cowbridge Garage), with whom I was friendly, used to come with us. Another friend was Margaret Jenkins of Cambrian House. The Jenkinses had a little brewery where the Vale of Glamorgan pub now is, and the man running their off-licence was Joe Staien. His father had stables at Coed Hills, near St Hilary.

Entertainments were held in the Town Hall, when the Vicar, Revd Isaiah Roberts, and Revd Davies the curate would run magic lantern shows.

When my parents lived at Eastfield House, we used to have a donkey cart, which would take about five or six of us. My sister and her friends used to go down to the Leys in that. I also liked horses, and enjoyed riding.

My parents were friendly with a lot of people in Llanblethian - Revd WF Evans, the former headmaster of the Grammar School, in St Quentin's, the Dunns in The Cross, the Thomases in Stallcourt (and before them the Williamses of the Bear, before they moved to Penllyn), and the Waymans in Brynhyfryd (they had lived at Brocastle before that). Other friends were the Morrises - he was the county surveyor - in Great House, Dai Cox in the farm on Broadway, Morgan at Cusop (he kept chickens in the field opposite), Gilbert Williams at the Vicarage and the Halls at Hill House.

Minnie Edmondes lived in Old Hall, and Mrs Davies the curate's wife lived in the east end; they and my mother used to meet to have a real good morning's gossip in the Misses Griffiths's shop in High Street, a gathering to get the talk of the town. Minnie Edmondes lived on her own, with staff, in Old Hall. Her sister married Lawrence Williams from Bonvilston, and their son, 'Tip' Williams, later lived in the Verlands.

Fred Williams, who owned the Bear Hotel, had earlier been farming in Penllyn - at Great House. He had six sons, including Evan, the jockey and Grand National winner, and John whom I married. Dr Meller across the road always wanted a son. I vaguely remember a poem in the *Glamorgan Gazette* on the death of Dr Meller . . .

Here lies the body of Charles Booth Meller,
when he was alive he was a hell of a feller
Marriage he left rather late in life,
he wanted a son but got four girls from his wife,
but across the way there were boys a-plenty

or some such rhyme.

There were three doctors here then - Dr Meller, who always wore a top hat and striped trousers, Torney who was living where Sorrento is now, and Dr Moynan who lived in Woodstock House. My brother, 'Dr Dai', took the practice over from Moynan, and my sister Susie kept house for him there before he married. He was in partnership with a cousin of mine, a John, and when the latter died on active service my brother took over the practice in Bridgend.

My husband and I followed his father in running the Bear; I was there for about ten years, between 1946 and 1956. It was a busy time, with some notable events. The Penllyn murder saw the Scotland Yard detective, 'Manning of the Yard', staying in the hotel, and also Lord Longford (then the Air Minister) stayed at the time of the Llandow air disaster.

JOYCE TONKIN, COWBRIDGE

Mrs Tonkin, née Sanders, spent nearly all her childhood in Cowbridge; her memories are essentially of the period between the First World War and 1932, when she moved to England. She now lives in a house on the edge of Stalling Down.

I was born on 8th July 1907 at the blacksmith's house in Pendoylan. My mother, Alice, had been in service at Penllyn Castle and then in Radyr. My father, John Sanders, was apprenticed to the blacksmith in St Nicholas, and my parents were married in Christ Church, Radyr. In fact, they were the first couple to be married there, and because of this they were given back their 7/6d licence fee. My grandfather managed the Vale of Glamorgan brewery which stood opposite the Duke of Wellington in Cowbridge. I was the eldest of four children, all girls – Joyce, Zena, Cynthia and Monica. Both Cynthia and Monica died before they reached the age of five and are buried in Cowbridge churchyard.

When I was six months old, we moved to Cowbridge, and lived in a house opposite the Police Station in Westgate, near the nonconformist chapel. We then moved to Town Mill and lived in the mill house (now Town Mill cottages); the mill was in ruins, but the old mill wheel was still there. The floor was rotten, and the Grammar School boys used to creep into the building to smoke. My father's smithy was in Eagle Lane, next to the old lodging house, where he concentrated on shoeing horses. On a few occasions he attended the Smithfield Show as a blacksmith, where he was highly commended. He also kept the hooves trimmed of the Hereford bulls which were shown by the better-off farmers, such as Owen Williams of Crossways, from 1916 onwards.

I remember the outbreak of the First World War, when the Glamorgan Yeomanry mustered on Stalling Down. Cowbridge was the gathering point for horses for the army before they were sent to France. The horses were

Arthur Mills's garage, 1910s, with the Cowbridge Arms to the right
and 42 High Street to the left

kept in the Market. My mother had seven soldiers of the Yeomanry billeted on her at a period during the war, each for a period of three months, before they were sent to France with the horses. I remember one Irishman, a regimental sergeant-major, who stayed for some time, and who made great use of the twenty-two public houses in Cowbridge.

My first school was on Broadway, Cowbridge. I remember Mr Sloman and Mr Harvey, who was a strict disciplinarian. There was also Mr Owen Phillips, who married Miss Baden, the Science teacher at the Girls' High School; they went to live at The Cairns in Llanblethian. I went on to the High School, where Mrs Forrester was the headteacher and Miss Gunter taught History and Geography. She lived opposite what became the cinema in Eastgate.

I left school at sixteen and went to Clark's College in Cardiff for a year. I caught the 7.45am train from Cowbridge, and on some occasions on the journey home I had to walk from Pontyclun because the train would not wait for the connection.

I then went to work at the Cowbridge Garage, in the High Street, next door but one to the Duke. I worked in the office for the owner, Mr Arthur Mills, who came from Cardiff and was an architect. He built the garage, and also bought the Cowbridge Arms next door, knocked it down and rebuilt it. That is where I had my office. He was the main Ford dealer, and used the front of the garage as his showroom; he also sold bikes as well as cars. Mr Mills became Mayor of Cowbridge four times. He had two children - Freda, four years older than me, and Clifford, who was younger. They kept two maids in their house, which occupied all the rooms above the garage; I used to stay to look after the house when the family went to their Porthcawl house for the summer. Mr Mills then built and opened the Pavilion cinema in Eastgate in September 1927, and I worked in the box office there. He wanted to open on Show Night (the Vale Show) but the work could not be finished in time. The first film shown in the cinema was 'This House of Vanity' and the films always played to crowded houses. The first films were of course silent, with a pianist, Gwyneth Evans; she married Oliver Jones, who was the film operator and one of the mechanics at the garage. Talkies were introduced when the cinema was sold to Phillips of Pontyclun. The Hunt Ball was always held in the ballroom of the cinema. This had a beautiful sprung maple floor.

I stopped working for Mr Mills when I married in 1932, and went to live in Gloucester, and then Leicester. I worked in the cash office of a munitions factory there during the war. I came back to Cowbridge at the end of the war because my mother needed help in the café she ran on the Downs. This was a little wooden hut, next door to O'Connor's Road House (today's Mughal Emperor). Mother did teas and cakes, and there was a tent at the back where the washing up was done. We then built the Richmond café across the road (now known as Norman's café) and also built Richmond House, where I now live, next door to it in 1957.

Before the war my sister Zena married Ivor Treharne, a corn and agricultural merchant, and they lived in Town Mill Road. Town Mill Road then was tree-lined with large gardens, and I remember my uncle Reg (Sanders) had bee hives there, near to the mill, and next to the river. Tom John, who had a brewery in Pentre in the Rhondda, lived in the Verlands, a lovely house with two or three fields attached. There was a large garden there in which Becky Jenkins's father worked. The Johns had two Daimlers; he kept a chauffeur for his wife, who would often be taken into the Dorothy café in Cardiff to buy half-a-dozen cakes. They had one married son, Maurice; every Monday morning Mrs John would stand by the gate of their drive waiting for a letter from her son.

Stan Treharne, the milkman, was Ivor Treharne's brother. He came from Penylan, and his wife's mother lived in the brewery house where the Vale of Glamorgan Inn is today, where my grandmother also used to live, and where I spent much time as a child. The bottling shop was where Dai John's clothing shop now is; the bottles of lemonade were sealed with glass marbles. The brewery was at the back – through the double doors at the side of the Vale. The owner, WL Jenkins, lived next door in Cambrian House. There was of course another brewery, owned by Lewis Jenkins, down near the river.

In Church Street, next door to 'Granny' Jenkins, lived John John, known to everyone as 'Johnny Grassy'. He was a diminutive man, a jaunty character who frequented all the hunt meets. He had a little white beard, used a thumb-stick, and always wore a bowler hat and breeches.

To celebrate the end of the war in November 1918, Dr Moynan of Woodstock House, opposite the Masons Arms, rolled a barrel of beer to the Town Hall. He was another man who always wore breeches.

I also remember Ma Haig, who lived in the almshouses in Llanblethian, coming into Cowbridge, always travelling in a donkey and cart. She liked a drink or two, and regularly went into the Railway Inn (now Basil's). The donkey always knew his way home! Sometimes however, when Ma was in the pub, the boys would untie the donkey and put him in the cart backwards, to amuse themselves and to see if Ma would notice.

One of the main events of my early childhood was the March Fair, when a parade of stallions took place at 2pm, from the Masons Arms to the Duke of Wellington. There was also a street fair, and a market, and roundabouts for the children.

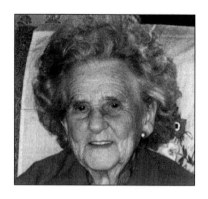

BECKY JENKINS, LLANBLETHIAN

Becky Jenkins's memories are of Llanblethian up to about 1926, when she went 'into service' in London. After some years there, she became nanny to Joanna Lewis, later Mrs Joanna Cory, and subsequently worked as a nanny for Sir Harry and Lady Llewellyn, looking after Roddy and Dai. Becky now lives in Llanblethian.

I was born on 11th June 1909 at 3 Greenfield Terrace, Llanblethian. Mother had thirteen children; two died young (George at six months, Mary at three years). The others were Ernest, Bill, Dick, John, Tom, Bert, Ada, Rachel, Peg, Dora, and of course, me.

My father, Thomas W Jenkins, like his father, was a 'horse man'. He worked in Dynevor Cottage with Dr and Mrs Shepherd, in the Verlands (with the Johns) and then moved to the Glamorgan Hunt stables as a head groom. Mr Chappell was the other head groom. Mr and Mrs Chappell drove into Cowbridge in a donkey cart from the stables. There was a lot of work there – hunting, as well as hiring out horses. Hunting was for the elite then; the Boxing Day meet on the Downs was especially popular. Father worked a long day – he didn't come home till 6 or 7pm. My mother did the washing for the stable boys. Father made liniment for horses, and it was used for the Jenkins children as well!

My grandmother on my mother's side was Rachel Fenimore. She married one of the Johns, so mother's name was Ada Johns. She had been in service with Lady Franklen at St Hilary.

My father's parents lived in a cottage opposite Cowbridge church (No 6 Church Street). Grandpa was a Crimean war veteran; he had been wounded, and was decorated for his service there. He had a little beard; I never kissed him – I was afraid of him! In their house, there was always a fire, banked well up, winter or summer. There was a row of brass candlesticks on the mantelpiece, and an old clock on the wall with looped chains. There was also a settle where I would sit and tell Gran the news.

Gran used to clean the church, and grandfather cleaned the churchyard, as a labour of love. Every week, Gran used to place bread for the poor on the offerings board in the church, just inside the door, and I used to help her.

All the family went to Llanblethian church; all six of my brothers used to blow the organ there, for 2/6d a year! We all went to church regularly; I've had the same seat in Llanblethian church since I was three. All thirteen children were christened: Revd Isaiah Roberts christened me, at the same time as Harry Thomas, Stallcourt.

I went to school on Broadway, Cowbridge; the school drew in children not only from Cowbridge and Llanblethian, but also from Llandough, Aberthin and some from Ystradowen. Mr Sloman was the teacher - we called him the German Jew, and we were all scared of him. One of the teachers, Mr Phillips, used to shout and throw chalk - he was a madman! Mr Roberts was much calmer; he eventually became headmaster, but he was first of all a class teacher, under Mr Sloman. Other teachers were Miss Lewis, Miss Ralls, Miss Mary Tutton, Miss Escott.

We grew up in Greenfield Terrace. The first house was occupied by Johnny John, then next-door were the Vaughans (Mrs Hilda Vaughan, large family, ten children), then us, then the Dixons in a one-up, one-down cottage. When Mrs Dixon died, and Violet Dixon left, father bought that cottage to give us more room. Upstairs in No 3, the big bedroom was like a dormitory. The house had a paved front, which was kept all scrubbed right up to the gate. We grew vegetables in the garden, and at the top of the garden was the privy. This had a tin roof - my brothers used to throw stones onto the roof just to make the occupants jump!

Near us in Llanblethian, at the bottom of Broadway Hill, were the almshouses, one of which was occupied by Ma Haig. She was an old Irish woman, who used to laugh and joke with children who were playing on the bridge. When she went in, boys would play tricks on her - tying a button onto cotton and using it to tap on the window - because they knew she'd rush out swearing. Next door was Mr Groom, a dear old man who looked like a tramp. He used to catch rabbits and skin them, and he slept on the floor. We used to love looking in through the windows to see him lying on his pile of sacks. Mother used to make cake for him, which we children would take round.

The small cottage near them (now a garden) was later known as Em Royal's cottage. That also had a tin roof, on which boys loved to throw stones - because of the noise - just to annoy the occupants. Ted and Mary

Becky Jenkins and her father outside Greenfield Terrace, Llanblethian

Surrey lived there, with their crippled daughter Mary Jane, who did a lot of sewing. Ted and Mary were always quarrelling.

In the other direction from our house were the bakehouse and the mill. Johnny and Jane Thomas lived in the bakehouse, with their daughters, Mabel and Flossie. The kitchen was always warm, as the bakehouse was off the kitchen. Johnny used to take bread in their trap (pulled by Polly, the horse) around Penllyn. As children, we went round with them – I remember going out with Mabel in the cart; she was always singing. She would stop at the entrance to the drive to Penllyn Castle, and I'd walk up to the castle with the bread. There were two sorts of bread - a tin loaf and a bottom loaf. The latter could be peeled off in layers and I remember doing just that on my walk to the castle.

Mr Spencer lived in the mill. One of his sons, Gilead Spencer, lived in the cottage opposite - Brook House. The mill was still working, and they had a bakehouse too.

We used to get our drinking water from the pump near the mill (or if that was frozen, we would have to go to the spring at Bowman's Well, which always flowed).

Today, Piccadilly is much altered from what it was in my childhood. People who lived there when I was young were old Mrs Chisell, Mrs Boobyer, Lil Jones and Mary Ann Williams. Mary Ann used to keep cows near the castle - she used to go up there every day with a bucket to milk them. Old man Jenkins also had a sweet shop in Piccadilly - boys always used to make him get jars from the top shelf just to make him go up and down.

Factory House also contained a sweet shop, run by another Jenkins family: the children were Vivian, Olive and Cissie. I have a vague memory of Welsh women, in their tall black hats and shawls coming down to the factory - perhaps to buy flannel.

I worked at Kingscombe Farm for three years or so, as 'head cook and bottlewasher', from when I left school at fourteen. Dick Jenkins, newly widowed, lived there with his daughter Ruby, and his mother Hannah. Initially, I worked mornings only, but it soon developed into a full day's work. It was hard work, not only the domestic chores, but also scrubbing out churns, and helping to make butter, 30lbs at a time. I didn't have much to do with Ruby, because Dick's cousin Martha, who lived in Rosedew (now Greystones) came to look after her, though Ruby did not take to her. Martha eventually married Dick Jenkins, and poor little Ruby died, some time after I left.

Kingscombe was a real old farmhouse, with rough stone-flagged floors. The windows today are still much as they were then. The house was divided into two: Dick had the back part, with a large front room for his mother, who was an invalid, and who only moved from chair to bed and back. The first thing I had to do in the house of a morning was to see to her needs. The remainder of the front of the house was let out to the Bassetts - Mrs Bassett, her daughter Hilda, who was a mistress in the High

School, and her son, and her mother-in-law, Mrs Renouf, a Jerseywoman and an old dear.

When I was seventeen I worked for a while at the Verlands, for the John family. Father was head groom to Tom John at that time. Every morning he would have to take Tom John to Cowbridge station, at 8am, in the brake with a high-stepping horse. They were so punctual that people used to set their clocks by him.

I always wanted to go to London – so many girls from our area went to work in London when they left school, and then they'd come back looking beautifully smart, and speaking well. Father wouldn't let me go until I was seventeen – and then only if my sister went with me. So, after working for some time at the Verlands, I persuaded my sister Rachel, who was four years older than I, to come with me. We both worked for the daughter of Sir Sydney and Lady Byass of Llandough Castle. Miss Mollie had been my guide leader at Llandough; she became Mrs Capt Hone, 160 Gloucester Terrace, London, and I was house parlour maid and Rachel was cook-general.

WINIFRED HUISH, ABERTHIN

Winifred Huish in The Limes, about 1916

Mrs Huish, née Burnage, still lives in the house in Aberthin into which her family moved in 1918. She deals here with Aberthin and Cowbridge from about the end of the First World War, and in a remarkable feat of memory has retraced her steps through Cowbridge - a town she knew well through helping her mother deliver newspapers - in the 1920s.

I moved from Mountain Ash, where I was born in 1912, to Cowbridge when I was a few months old. (My grandparents, my mother's parents, were from Trerhyngyll.) After living in the Limes for a few years, my mother, Mrs Burnage, rented a cottage in Aberthin belonging to Llanblethian church in 1918. It had to be re-thatched before our family - mother, two boys, two girls - moved in. This is the cottage in which I live today.

My mother kept three or four cows, some pigs, chickens and geese. We rented land from various farmers, and the cattle also used to graze on the common, and on the verges of the lane going past the house up to the Cardiff road near Cowbridge, when they were being taken to their field. It was my job to make sure the cattle wouldn't get on to the Cardiff road. The cows were kept for milk, cheese and butter. The cheese was made in one of the two rooms of the cottage - we heated the milk to blood heat, put rennet in it, and let it settle in an earthenware pan, with a muslin cloth on top, and with a saucer put on the cloth. We'd skim the whey off the cheese into the saucer. When the cheese was ready, we'd mix it with salt or sage - that was very tasty, the sage cheese. It was a white, creamy, Welsh cheese. We made enough for ourselves, sometimes with enough left over to sell, and we also made butter for customers. The pigs were killed for bacon and pork - I can remember the bacon hanging from the rafters - and the pork was for home and sometimes for customers in Cowbridge. The calves were reared for veal mostly. Dai Escott, the Cowbridge butcher, would often say 'keep that one for me'; and they would also be taken to markets at Ystradowen (this was a big market, held opposite the White Lion), at Peterston, or at Cowbridge. Tom Thomas of Stallcourt was a big cattle dealer, and he would often buy cattle off the fields, and get drovers to drive them to Stallcourt or to his other fields to finish them off; I can remember that we also sold a lot to Harry Thomas, his son.

We would tend to graze one field, and keep the next for hay for winter feed. When we made a mow of hay, the boys would go down into the Marriage, the marshy land near the river, and cut reeds to make a thatch for the haymow.

As well as the bigger farmers, quite a few people in Aberthin kept one or two cows for their own use. Pant Wilkin, kept by Frank Rose, had fields stretching up towards Welsh St Donats, and Llanquian, kept by Watkins, had a few fields going up to Hatches Lane, the back road to Welsh St Donats. Similarly, John Radcliffe at Sweetings (he had bought the farm from the Yorwerths) had land where Downs View Close and the Spinney is today. The other farmers drove their cows through the village to find grazing. Bill Jones at Paradwys used to bring them to our lane or on to the Cardiff road; the Thomases at Cartref brought them to the Slade or to a field on the top of the common; Miss May Collier of Brynhyfryd, who used to sell milk, brought her animals through the village to fields behind Maes Lloi. The Fredericks at Court Farm used to go up Hatches Lane but also on to the common, while Alice Williams, and later the Bowens, at Aberthin House, drove the cattle through the village to the meadows reached via the Cowbridge road, over the Marriage near the river Thaw. Bill Richards at Penylan, who had land on the Maendy road, used to take his cows as far as Newton Cross, and also along the road to Cowbridge where the school is today.

I remember that on six days a week, Jones Paradwys took his milk to Maendy platform to be sent by rail to the main line at Llantrisant; on Sunday mornings, he'd have to take the milk to Llantrisant as there were no trains on the Cowbridge line. All this stopped, of course, once lorries started collecting the milk, and the churns would be left at the roadside to be collected.

Aberthin House was one of the bigger farms, but for much of the time Alice Williams – previously Alice Lane – rented out her land; we rented

Eastgate, 1908

some of her fields. Early on, Mrs Williams took in lodgers there, such as Mr Roberts from Broadway School, and some masters from the Grammar School. It was then bought by Rees of Penmark for his daughter, who had married Aubrey Bowen. The farmyard was in what is now called The Orchard. Near the stream were cottages which were used as farm buildings, while the orchard proper was near the Hatches lane. When Mr Frederick of Court Farm bought Aberthin House in about 1938, he rented it out, but kept the farmyard and built a hay barn there. When I was very young, the Yorwerths owned River Row and Sweetings. Ted Rue who was farming in Trebettin bought the Row in the 1920s, and lived in one of the five houses; the Fredericks eventually bought those too.

The first people I can remember in Great House were old Mr and Mrs Hughes. Mr Hughes had land in the Perrogs, the sloping land on the Cowbridge side of Stalling Down, and in Cae Mawr and the Maes meadows behind Cae Lloi, but I can't remember him with cattle. He used to keep huge cart horses and farm implements in his barn on the Llanquian road. Then George John, who had been born in the village but had moved away, wanted to return, so he bought the barn and converted it into a house in about 1920. The Fredericks also bought this after Mr and Mrs John died, in about 1940.

In 1924, my mother bought the farmyard in the middle of the village (next to the Hare and Hounds) at the Owen Williams sale, when the whole Crossways estate was broken up, and we used it as our farmyard after that.

Unusually for the village children, my sister and I (and three others) went to school in Cowbridge, on Broadway, rather than to Maendy. Among my teachers were Mr Frederick (from Court Farm), Miss Doris Miles (Mrs Buchalik), the Misses Kate and Mary Tutton, Miss Dolly Williams and Mr Sloman the headmaster. I left at the age of fourteen, and came home to work. I used to carry water from the pump near the chapel, one of three pumps in the village (the others were on the common opposite Penylan, and on the Llanquian road near Crud yr Awel; there was also a water spout near Brewery Cottage). I also used to deliver newspapers, because my mother had the agency (from 1913 to 1943) for the *Echo* and for all the Sunday papers. I delivered newspapers from the time I was in a Welsh shawl in my mother's arms; and later when I was transported in a push chair, in the pony and trap, and on the crossbar of my brother's bike.

On Sundays, we – mother, me and my brother Jack – would go at about 5.30 or 6.00am, come rain or shine, in our pony and trap to fetch the newspapers from Llantrisant station. Then we delivered them to Rhydhalog Farm, just out of Talygarn, to Ystradowen, Trerhyngyll, Maendy (where we'd leave the papers for Prisk, to be collected), Welsh St Donats, Aberthin and Cowbridge, and then on by pushbike to Llanblethian. I think I knocked every door in Cowbridge – I could never play 'Knock, knock', because everybody recognised my knock.

Mother never had a shop but, after 1943, my brother Jack's wife took over the agency and then started a shop in Cowbridge. That was in the building now used by Thresher's and where Colin Campbell, who had lost a leg in the war, had a greengrocery and teashop and also sold ice cream. The Reynolds family took over the larger shop for a time; their ice cream was out of this world! Later Jack moved to his shop where Nicholas the butcher is today.

Because I delivered newspapers all over Cowbridge, I can remember all the shops and pubs of Cowbridge of my youth. I only went into the pubs to deliver the papers. Starting at the east end, there was the Crown and

Anchor where the landlady was Mrs Raymond, the Phillipses in the Edmondes Arms, and Mr Denbury in the Railway, where Basil's is today. The Commercial was run by the Powers, and then the Pughs. Mr Pugh was a celebrated water diviner - he located water in Llanharry, from which they ran a pipeline past Efail Roper, Pencyrn and Aberthin to Cowbridge. Mrs Annie Thomas was landlady of the Druids next to the railway station. The Ancient Druid was not a pub in those days; that's where Colin Adams was born. In the Wheelwright's Arms (which was where the cinema was built) was the Aubrey family, and then in the Bridge Inn (today's Bookshop) was Granny Crowley. The Fitzgeralds were in the Blue Bell, and Mrs Hayter ran the Horse and Groom - her husband was a carpenter. Mrs Thomas was in the Butchers Arms, and in the Royal Oak (Gaskell and Walker's today) was Viv John, who later went to the Aubrey Arms in Bonvilston. Opposite, in the Boar's Head, was Mr Upshall who had some land opposite the new school in Aberthin road, with a garden with apple trees in it. The White Lion next door was run by Mrs Villis. On the other side of the road, Mrs Labdon ran the Cowbridge Arms and, next door, Spencer was in the Duke before Tom Pratt. Then there was the Bear, Mr Cross in the Masons Arms, Mrs Morgans in the Bush, Mrs Llewellyn in the Pelican opposite (now the Tack Shop), Mrs Villis in the Greyhound in Westgate and finally Mrs Russell in the Westgate Inn.

As far as the shops were concerned, there was Fred Wadham in Eastgate (he used to live on Penylan Hill at Brynhowell), then next to the old Post Office, where the PO yard is now, was Daisy Stone's little sweet shop. She'd sell sugar and tea and pop and sweets. We used to leave our bikes at the back of the shop when we went to the cinema - lots of us, youngsters from Welsh St Donats and Maendy too. Then there was Lewis's shop (in Kumalo) selling fruit and wet fish. They were the grandparents of Bill Lewis the fire officer. A visiting dentist, Morgan, would also hold a surgery at their house in the late 1920s. The Chisells had a sweet shop where the hairdresser is today, and then on the corner of Bethuel's Court was Tucker's ironmongery, where we used to buy paraffin. Next came Thomas the butcher, and then where the Council offices are, Pickards - who retired to Rock House at the west end of town - sold china. Catherine David, an aunt of Billy Llewellyn the rugby player, ran a shoe shop in the big building of 87 Eastgate; she was followed there by the Mustoes, and then by Nurse Rymer. The latter had been a district nurse living across the road and who had gone on her rounds in a donkey cart. She then opened a

Mrs Webb's shop, 30 High Street, 1936

maternity home on the first floor of No 87, and turned the ground floor into a little tearoom and cake shop, selling sponge and fancy cakes. It was popularly known as Maudie's, named after her housekeeper/companion and sister Maud Hutchings. John Williams the draper in London House was the last shop in the east end.

On the other side of Eastgate, Billy David the butcher opened a shop next to the Commercial Hotel (and had Bill Oakley, who later opened his own shop next to Bird's, as an apprentice); on the corner with Croft Street was Fitzgerald's china shop. Rhoscelyn was a private house, lived in by a Mrs Thomas, then came Bob Thomas the baker (later to be known as Bob the bus) in the premises until fairly recently used by Thomas Bros, funeral directors. The shop and bakehouse were bought by Liscombes of Llantrithyd, and then Mrs Watts looked after the shop and did the baking. When we lived in the Limes, mother always used to make her own bread, and we'd take the tins of dough, and yeast cake and seed cake to Bob the baker for him to bake them for us. Through the double doors was the only bakehouse in Cowbridge in those days – and it was a big one. The baker used a flat shovel with a long handle to put the tins in and take the tins out of the oven, because the heat was so intense.

After the Wesleyan chapel came two private houses, the Giles family living in Heath House, then today's Gwyn House had Gwyn and Gwyn's office in the left-hand side of the building, and Nurse Rymer's home on the right-hand side. Hobson the vet had his lodgings here. Next to the Wheelwright's Arms, Billy Arnott and his sister Elsie had a draper's shop (in the building where Brown's later had a bookshop, next door to Brown's printing works). Then came Arthur Thomas the butcher, with a marble window sill, Mrs Maddox's chip shop and then the Bridge Inn. On this side of the bridge, adjoining Evans's garage, was Arnold's china shop, later Tucker's.

Over the bridge on the other side of the road was Charlie Davies the barber, and then Fitzgerald's cake shop; she had tins of yeast cake, seed cake, and bread pudding – with pastry top and bottom and bread with fruit in it between, as brown as a nut. Opposite, after the Blue Bell, was the garage where Mr Maddox kept his bus, for outings to places like Tintern Abbey – I remember it spitting and spluttering as it went off. Later on, this became the Post Office garage for their motor bikes. The Miles family had the next house, with a grocer's on the left-hand side, and a record shop, run by Bertie Miles in the room on the right. The next low building was Nelson Andrews's shoe shop; he was an uncle to Flo Golden, who became Mayor of Cowbridge. Victor Grubb the barber, from Red House in Maendy, took over after Andrews.

After the lane to Bird's yard was a small shop used by Phillips the plumber; it later became Tom Whitney's butcher's shop. He had earlier farmed at Mount Pleasant. Billy Batt, also to be Mayor of Cowbridge, lived in the cottage at the back. Bird's the ironmongers was followed by Mrs Davies the paper shop (and Glyn Davies also sold records there), Watkins the tailor, and, after the Royal Oak, Checketts the shoemaker – and when the Checketts moved to Mrs Chisell's old shop in Eastgate, Dai Escott came in as a butcher. A number of ex-servicemen, like Mr Escott, came in and started businesses in the first available premises, and then moved on to more suitable premises later – Escotts moved across the road to where Sanders's shoe shop is today.

Gwyn Lewis moved to the first house after the archway, when Elsie and Bert Griffiths left it to go to the Horse and Groom. He had a wet-fish delivery round, and then started a fish and chip shop there and Horace Lewis (no relation) took it over in the early 1930s. Next door were the Lanes, who had moved from 6 Westgate. A dentist from Bridgend came to set up a surgery once a week (in the 1920s); Jim Lane's daughter married the dentist. She was a cousin of Eddie John, so it is not surprising that Eddie's father, Willie John the Eagle, retired to live here during the last war, and was looked after by his daughter Avis (who married Glyn Williams the County Librarian). Cowbridge is a family affair!

Charlie Davies the Buns was a confectioner in the building where the Ogmore Vale bakery is today. He was followed here by Mrs Webb who ran a grocery store; her husband was Harry Webb the blacksmith whose forge was in Bear Lane. The left-hand side of Great House was a private house; Mr Evans the chemist occupied the right-hand side, then in about 1920 he was succeeded by Reg Williams when he too came out of the army. My mother used to go to Mr Williams for eye tests. On the other side of the arch was another chemist, John Williams; then Miss Gibbs the newsagent, Reynolds's grocery shop, and Mills's garage. Just in Church Street was Thomas the saddlers, and on the corner was WE Jones's cycle shop, with a long window for display. Hayter's photographic studios were upstairs; later the downstairs property was taken over by Westcott the barber. Next door, Mrs Mitchell's shop sold everything, then came Summerfield the greengrocer. The next building (Farthings today) was Davies's paper and paint shop, later split so that Flo Golden had her confectioner's shop on the left and Thomas and Evans cake shop, run by Molly Palmer, was on the right.

The next buildings were the garage of Jones Pentwyn, Dr Meller's house, Ollie Jones's garage, and then the Bank. The young Edmondes family was in Old Hall; old Mrs Edmondes had moved to St Hilary. We had no contact with them, but they had lots of staff: grooms and gardeners as well as house servants.

On the other side of the road, after the Town Hall came Miles the solicitor in Taynton House, Mrs Upshall the Boar's Head, which became Ryans the saddlers, and then the White Lion which was run by Mrs Villis. When she gave up the licence, her niece Kathleen, who had been brought up by her aunt and had married Bert Rustell, opened a greengrocery there. Dai Escott moved from across the road to Miss Thomas's shop in No 29, and then Maud Escott opened a fish and chip shop there. I hear this is still causing problems when people try to redecorate the wall where the frier was located! Next to Arthur Sanders's shoe shop was David Williams the grocer (in today's Lloyds TSB Bank), and then came John David the auctioneer's office (the forerunner of Watts and Morgan). I remember the Co-op opening in the next building in the 1920s, then Fred Evans the draper was in No 39. This was a gentlemen's tailors - he had Mr Williams the tailor (who lived in Sunnyside, on the Bridge) and Mr Marks, the organist, working for him. When Fred Evans retired, Mr Marks carried on his tailoring business in his own house in 16 Eastgate; this must have been about the time of the last war.

A private house, Ty Hen, with railings outside, came next. Webb the blacksmith lived there till he moved to the house next to Sorrento. Then came Arthur John's shop, then Miss Griffiths's grocer shop where I used to stand outside to smell the coffee. The other side of the arch, Alfred James's china shop was replaced by Boots's shoe shop where Miss Lena Barker from Borough Close worked. The brewery was next, but I can't remember it in operation; then David the thatcher, who thatched the little house for the Queen, lived in what is today the Vale of Glamorgan Inn. Cambrian House, double-fronted, was where Willie Jenkins the Brewery lived; his daughter married Gilbert Williams the vicar of Llanblethian and Bonvilston. John Thomas the draper had the next shop, then came the Midland Bank, managed by Robert Thomas, in the building which is today HR Thomas, estate agents. In what is now the HSBC Bank was Bob Morgan the butcher, who moved to Eastgate when the bank bought the premises.

I can picture the Williams family of the Bear of an evening, the boys standing in the doorway with their hands in their pockets, with their father. He was from Penllyn; Mrs Williams was a Thomas of Stallcourt. Then came Tom Yorwerth's house and office. He was the agent for Owen Williams of Crossways, as well as being an auctioneer. Frank Cross and Len James of Cross Inn had their apprenticeship with him. Tom Yorwerth's brother William owned property in Aberthin, and a plaque in Aberthin chapel records the conversion of a stable into the vestry in 1924/5, officially opened by William Yorwerth. Dr Hastings Torney lived in Sorrento, and had his surgery there; Jack Thomas the draper lived next door. Then came the house where Evans the solicitor lived (brother of Fred Evans the draper, and Arthur Evans of the Garage), and then the little house on the corner - where later Trevor and Molly Williams used to live - belonged to Old Hall opposite and was occupied by gardeners or servants of Old Hall. The Overtons were there - but when he left Old Hall to go to work on the railway, Mr Overton had to move, and went to live in the west end, next door to Mr Croome the chimney sweep.

On the other side of Cooper's Lane was where Jim Lewis the cooper lived, with all his beer barrels, cider barrels, and cheese vats - those with the central drainage holes - standing outside. I remember him clearly, a nice old gentleman, quiet, busy with his work. His work was his life. He lived and slept in his workroom, as did many craftspeople in those days. It was very dark, lit only by candlelight or paraffin lamps. You had to go down steps into his workroom, and he'd be there surrounded by his tools and his wood. He used the building behind (later to be Eddie John's grain store) to keep most of his wood. Annie Overton from across the way used to run errands for him. Further down Cooper's Lane was David Tilley's carpentry shop. He was a beautiful furniture maker and a carriage maker too. There would usually be cart wheels ranged on the wall on the left-hand side of Cooper's Lane waiting to have new spokes or hubs inserted. His saw pit was in the open space opposite, near the little cottage opening on to Bear Lane where Henry Trott, a plate-layer on the railway, lived. In those days Cowbridge people were either post or railway or business people.

Back to the High Street: Llwyncelyn was where Mr David the auctioneer lived; next came Lydia Davies's shop - she was the mother of Mrs Caines who ran the shop for many years. William Pickard, his wife and three daughters lived in the next house, and continued to do so when the front part became Watts and Morgan's offices. He also wrote for the *Glamorgan Gazette* under the pen name of Velox; of the daughters, Elsie became Mrs Trotman, and Ethel became Mrs Roberts, whose son Glyn ran the delicatessen where Thresher's is today. Finally, Dr Moynan lived in Woodstock House, and was followed there by Dr Dai Evans.

In the Butts were three cottages, old-fashioned, with low ceilings. Their living rooms opened onto the street. In the first lived the two Miss Eddolls, who used to leave their side window slightly open for me to push the newspaper through; the second changed hands a lot - I remember the Trews, and then Percy Fitzgerald, living there; in the third were the Jenkinses.

Among the people living on the south side of Westgate were Jim Croome the sweep in No 8, Dr Gallaher in Stafford House (in partnership with Dr Jenkins from Pontyclun) to be followed by Dr Browne Millar, and

DC Watts (of Watts and Morgan) in West House, before he built West Winds on Love Lane. Right at the far end, beyond Mrs Villis's house where she kept a little sweetshop after she gave up the licence for the Greyhound, were two houses, John Bond's cottage and Rock House, where George Pickard lived.

The first building on the north side of Westgate was the Eagle agricultural stores, run by Willie John, the son of the founder of the firm, Edward John. Willie also lived there: this was a sizeable building. Across the narrow lane was the Pelican, soon to be converted into a house. Mr Davies the saddler (husband of Lydia Davies) had his workshop next door, in what became Mr Deaves's house; then came Harry Collings, the watch and clock repairer, who used his front room, only dimly lit by candle or gas light, as his workshop. After the next house was a large garden. I can remember Dorothy Jenkins's parents, who lived in the Butts, building their bungalow here. He was a carpenter, who must have worked in the joinery in Pontyclun as I remember him coming off the train with his bag of tools on his shoulder. He built the bungalow in the evenings, after work. Dorothy married Mervyn Evans from Sweetings in Aberthin, and they lived here later. (The bungalow has recently been replaced by four town houses.)

On the other side of the Broad Shoard, Phillips the plumber lived in the first house; then came a long wall (where, apparently there'd been thatched cottages before) and where Billy Llewellyn from Bridgend built three houses. Davies the Pop lived in the first, Len Rowsell, the baker for Harry Gibbs, in the second, and the Mustoes, who had moved from Eastgate, in the third. After the Baptist chapel came Mrs Lewis's sweet and paper shop. Her son George was a driver on the railway; Billy was a railway fireman, but could not continue after he broke his leg, and so became stationmaster at Ystradowen. After the death of Mrs Lewis, the house was occupied by the caretaker for the Baptist chapel. Mrs Trew's house came next to David Tilley in Ivy House, and then Gwyneth and Tom Carter lived in the last of the houses; when they left, Johnson Miles came there.

There was then a field, in which houses and bungalows were gradually built, before you came to three thatched cottages, occupied by the Seviours (whose children moved to live on Broadway), Granny Griffiths in the middle one – the old tollgate house which had a porch sticking out – and then Mrs Clements. These three houses had their gardens opposite, in Hopyard Meadow. The last two houses in Westgate were the Westgate

Inn, run by Mrs Russell, who sold sweets and chocolate when she gave up the licence, and Thorn Villa, where John Roberts the Ystradowen timber merchant lived.

There have been very great changes in life in Aberthin and Cowbridge within my memory. I can remember piped water coming in, in 1926, and electricity a year later. The linesmen for the electricity kept their reels of wire and tools in the outhouses of the Farmers Arms in Aberthin. Most of them came from Ely, and came in by train as far as Maendy halt. They then walked to Aberthin, picking up snails from the walls as they came, and then proceeded to boil these up for their breakfast, which revolted us children.

So many people used to travel by pony and trap, or dray, or gig, or whatever: not only Nurse Rymer with her donkey and governess cart, but Mrs Sharpe from Welsh St Donats with her donkey and small cart, Mr Thomas the relieving officer in his pony and trap, Llewellyn of Moorlands in his governess trap coming in to do the Friday shopping, and many more. Tom Whitney, and later the Goldsworthys, from Mount Pleasant used to deliver their milk with their pony and dray, but I also remember Mark Roberts from Eastgate walking on his milk round using a yoke, with two jacks hanging from it. Old Mrs Edmunds from the first old house in Broadway, now disappeared and replaced by two modern ones (next to Basil's car park), had a little hand trolley with buckets, jacks and measures. She used to sell milk and cream - she had land at the Cardiff road end of our lane where she kept a couple of cows and chickens, and night and morning she would walk up there to milk the cows in the fields.

Another memory linked with cattle was seeing Owen Williams's prize Herefords, which had been walked down from Crossways, being paraded through Cowbridge. They were beautiful animals, on their way to the railway station, being taken to some show or other.

HUBERT THOMAS, LLANBLETHIAN, LLYSWORNEY AND COWBRIDGE

Hubert Thomas, born in Llanblethian, brought up in Llanblethian and Llysworney, worked for forty-one years for Cowbridge RDC, as Public Health Officer. Here, he remembers aspects of his life up to the end of the Second World War.

I was born in Llanblethian Farm in 1916. I remember my mother saying that Mrs Hancock from Llysworney had acted as midwife. She had attended my mother when my sister was born, so my father got the pony and trap out to go to Llysworney to get Mrs Hancock to be present at my birth.

The Carnes of Nash Manor owned both Llanblethian Farm and Great House, opposite. My sister Vera had indifferent health, and so the Carnes promised my parents that they could have Great House, which was drier and a better building, when Mr Durston the butcher ended his lease. Two memories of living in Great House - pushing my brother Alan in his pram into the river, accidentally of course, and being operated on by a surgeon and nurse from Cardiff, in my father's bedroom, when they removed a TB gland in my neck. I was home from school (the Junior school on Broadway) for three months after that. I also remember my first day at school - being driven there in the horse and trap by my father and Dai Cox, who had Broadway Farm, and then Miss Rees the Infants' school headmistress welcoming me with a toy giraffe - I went in quite eagerly, like a lamb to the slaughter.

We moved to Penyrheol Farm in Llysworney in 1925. This was my mother's family home; she too was a Thomas. Three of the sons of the farm had gone out to the United States after the Civil War - William, a reporter on the *Glamorgan Gazette* (and whose letters home are now in the Glamorgan Record Office), Thomas who later farmed West Farm in Wick, and David who was the most successful in America. David came back to farm Stallcourt in Llanblethian, and was murdered for his money on Llanblethian Hill in 1886.

When we were at Llysworney, and after I had started at the Grammar School, I had to have another operation, this time on my chest. This was on the advice of Dr Dai (Evans, father of Blair Evans of Llancarfan). The operation was carried out in the Cottage Hospital in Bridgend, and this time I had to spend two terms at home, recuperating. I had fallen so far behind in school that it was decided I should leave, and my father got me to spend the next year on the farm. These were hard times, and farming was at a low ebb - I remember taking a dray full of lambs to Llantwit Major market one week, and we were only offered 27/6d for them. 'Take them home', my father said - only to find that the next week the price had fallen to 25/-.

In 1933, I started as a junior clerk in the Health department of the Council Offices in Eastgate. This building had been converted from Pickard's grocery shop in 1924. I started a correspondence course - and was helped in my maths by Mr McAdam from the Grammar School, a lovely man. On passing this, I went on to a Public Health course in Cardiff, for which I was given a half-day off a week. When I went up to London for the exams, I stayed with the nephew of Nurse Rawnsley, the health visitor who worked with us; she was firm, but very kind. The results were posted on the board at the offices of the Royal Sanitary Institution, and my cousin Kate who lived in London sent me a telegram to say that I had passed. I was so excited that I gave the telegraph boy 2/6d, a princely sum in those days!

When my father died in 1938, my mother continued at the farm for a short time, and then my sister and her husband took it over. We then moved to the house we had had built at the Nash corner close to Llysworney. Though there was a cricket field behind the council houses, and a soccer team too, I didn't play much sport, except for tennis on the court belonging to the old Llysworney school teacher. I'd go to the cinema in Cowbridge, but more often Alan and I would walk to Pentre Meyrick to catch the bus to Bridgend, where we'd go to the cinema, have a pint, and finish the evening with fish and chips.

When the war started, and there was danger of air raids, Mrs Carne offered my mother and my sisters (but not Alan and me) the chance to share the cellar in Nash Manor. I recall the nearest bomb to fall very clearly. The air raid warning had sounded, and Alan and I were alone in the house. We looked out and saw a parachute coming down slowly - and then realised that there was a bomb attached to it. It fell in the copse before Sheepleys Close, on the Llantwit road near to the manor. It caused some damage to the pigeon house in Nash Manor grounds. The next day we went to inspect the damage, and found some of the nylon ropes which had been used to attach the parachute. I cut some off and for some years used the piece to tie up my dressing gown.

I also remember seeing the glare in the sky when incendiary bombs were dropped on Aberthin Road in Cowbridge.

Whereas Alan was in the Home Guard, and then in the RAF, I had been classified as grade III, unfit for service, because I'd had TB. We had several people billeted on us - Nurse Rawnsley was the billeting officer. The first evacuees came by train to Cardiff, then by bus to Cowbridge. They were taken to the cinema and sorted out there; we had a mother and her children, but they did not stay in the area long. Afterwards RAF officers were billeted on mother - that's where I learned to play three-handed bridge.

Pat and I got married in 1943. Arthur Gwyn, the Town Clerk, divided his mother's house next to the Council Offices into two, so that we could live there and keep an eye on his mother. I was conveniently close to my work. One of my duties at that time was arranging for the repairs of air raid damage in all the Cowbridge RDC area; this was much more wide-ranging than many people think. Cowbridge got off fairly lightly, but the Brynna-Llanharan area, in the north, had quite a lot of damage, and St Athan in the south was badly hit on a number of occasions.

I worked for forty-one years with Cowbridge RDC, and have fond memories of many of the councillors and of my colleagues. Richard Morgan, chairman of the Council, farmed in St Hilary; other farmers were Richards of Brigam, and Llewellyn Jenkins. The latter, who enjoyed a pint, would frequently go to the Bear after meetings. He kept his old dilapidated van in the brewery yard, and as a JP could always get the services of the policeman to push-start the van, no matter how many pints he had drunk! Joe David from Llanharan, also later to be chairman of the Council, was a very kind man; he would always look after Jack Jenkins, a Llanharan coalminer, when they went on conferences.

The council was always short of money - the only way that Dai Jones, the rate collector, could get any floor covering for his room was to claim that coins were falling through cracks in the floor - and then the lino which was provided only covered the area under the table. I can remember another rate and rent collector hiding in the stationery cupboard when a certain young lady called in to try to see him! Happy times!

BERTRAM JENKINS, LLANBLETHIAN

Bert Jenkins, Becky's brother, was born and brought up in Llanblethian. On leaving school he worked for the Post Office, and now lives in retirement in Porthcawl. These extracts from his reminiscences - written originally for his family - deal with Llanblethian in the period 1920 to 1936.

I was the youngest of a family of thirteen children, though a brother and a sister had died before I was born. The surviving children consisted of six boys and five girls. By today's standards, eleven children is a large family, but there was another large family in the village in those days, the Jameses: there were ten of them. The nurse present at my birth was Nurse Rymer of Cowbridge, a very small lady, always prim and proper in her uniform, and always with a white bonnet. She went on her visits in a donkey cart. She kept the donkey originally in what is now the Council Twt children's playground, but later she owned a shed on what is now the school's cricket field.

When I was about three years old I started going to Sunday school, and also became a choirboy in Llanblethian church. We also used to go to the Baptist school on Wednesday evenings. However, I recall that about six months earlier, my mother started to send me on washdays to the Council school on Broadway, which is now Ysgol Iolo Morganwg. I used to accompany my brother Dick and his friend Harry Thomas who were then in standard IV. Their class teacher, Mr Owen Phillips, had told my mother that she could send me to school with Dick on any day when she was busy with her housework. Because of this I must have started school unofficially when I was less than three years old!

I well remember my first proper day in school, in the Infants' class taught by Miss Rees. We then progressed to Miss Aubrey's class. We were expected to know the alphabet and be able to read fairly well before we entered Standard I which was taken by Miss Parker. Class II was taken by Miss Davies and later by Miss Gwyneth Thomas who was the daughter of Mr Thomas, the Relieving Officer for the Parish Help.

I was a good scholar and could read and write quite well before I entered Standard III where we were taught by Mr Willy Frederick. He was an ex-serviceman and was an excellent teacher. His family lived in Court Farm in Aberthin. Because I was a good reader Mr Frederick used to put me at the back of the class with three older boys who were unable to read. I taught them every time we had reading periods. I then went on to Standards IV and V. These were two classes, which were taught in the same room by Mr Roberts who was also an ex-serviceman. Although he was also a good teacher he was a bit heavy with his use of the cane. This was especially true in the handwriting lessons, if we did not write with the pen sloping over our right shoulders. The first we would know of our error was when we would receive a sharp crack across the knuckles of our writing hands. We never forgot those lessons!

Mr Frederick taught the boys gardening. The school owned a plot of land at the back, which was split up into small plots. For the last one and a half years of my schooling, when I was in Standard VI, my teacher was Mr Sloman. He was the headmaster and lived in the schoolhouse, which adjoined the school. His wife suffered from poor health and I remember that when I was in the Infants' class, a few of us used to go to her bedroom once a week to sing to her.

Once or twice a week during spring and summer, on fine afternoons, Classes II and III would be taken for a long walk along the roads and lanes, where the teacher would show us all the different wild flowers and birds in the hedgerows. We always looked forward to this.

The council had made open air swimming baths on the river Thaw at the back of the Town Hall in Cowbridge. There were covered cubicles to change in but the baths themselves were in the open air. The river water was very cold indeed. They used to say that there were fifteen springs feeding the water, which made it so very cold. We were taught to swim there. Each school, including the Girls' High School and the Grammar School, was allocated one afternoon a week in the baths, but no mixed bathing was allowed. If we went with the school we were given a season ticket for the baths free of charge. I have still got mine, in good condition after all these years!

On St David's Day we had a half day's holiday from school. The morning session was given over to the performing of plays in Welsh and the singing of Welsh songs. Of course, all the boys wore the famous leek, which we had to eat at the end of the morning! Needless to say we all wore the smallest leeks we could find.

Bert Jenkins and Dinkie outside Greenfield Terrace, Llanblethian, 1931

When I was eleven years old I sat the eleven-plus examinations. I passed and was allocated a place in Cowbridge Grammar School. Because my parents were not very well off, however, I was unable to take up the place.

They could have applied for financial help, but did not want 'charity'. I did not mind not being able to attend the grammar school.

I left school in 1932 at the age of fourteen. I had already done some relief work to allow one of the telegram boys to play cricket, and a full-time job came up as a telegram (or messenger) boy two weeks before I was due to leave school. Mr Sloman, the headmaster, marked me sick for the last two weeks so that I could take up the job. So I became a telegram boy for the GPO, for the area covered from Pendoylan through Llantrithyd to Llandow. There was an average of 300 telegrams a week coming through Cowbridge, and my hours of work were from 9.30am to 7.30pm Monday to Saturday, plus one and a half hours on Sunday morning. My wages were 9/3d, with 6d for Sunday - poor even in those days. Our uniform was almost military, with a pill-box hat and a navy-blue jacket and trousers; the buttons of the jacket had to be shining, and the trousers had to have sharp creases in them. We were inspected by the postmaster.

★★★

As I look back to my childhood and my teenage years, I am very aware as to how hard life was for my mother. I have vivid memories of washdays, which were usually on a Monday. I recall a huge bucket of dirty clothes soaking in rainwater, which had been collected in three huge wooden casks. These casks were sited by the back door where they could catch the water running from the roof. My mother would lift the bucket of clothes on to an open-hearth fire in the living room to boil. Then she would lift the hot bucket off the fire and pour the contents in to a large galvanised bath on the table in the back kitchen, so that she could hand wash the clothes. Each washday this process would be repeated about three times. After washing, the clothes would be wrung by hand and then put through a mangle. This had a wheel, which turned two wooden rollers. These would press together forcing the water out. The damp washing was then hung out to dry on the clothes line in the back garden. This process would be followed by arduous hours of ironing, using an old flat iron that was heated on the fire. We did not have any electricity in the house, so no washing machines, no spin dryers and no electric irons. In those days washing day was physically very hard work.

Before piped water came to the village we had to carry all drinking water from the public hand pump near the mill. It is still standing there today. There is also another pump near the church hall. Fetching water from the mill pump was a twice-daily job, mornings before school, and after school in the evenings. This job was always handed down to the youngest members of the family as soon as they had grown strong enough!

I had to fetch milk from the cowshed at Kingscombe Farm twice a day. The milk was measured out into a tin in the cowshed. I also used to fetch milk from Mrs Williams of Greenfield in the evenings. On Saturday mornings I fetched the milk from the dairy in Kingscombe Farm, as well as a big enamel jug full of buttermilk for my mother's weekly cake baking session. Also, we were given a half-pound of lovely farmhouse butter, which I earned by turning the handle of a gadget called a separator. This separated the cream from the milk, leaving what is known as skimmed milk, and the cream of the milk.

Every Thursday, and quite often on another day as well, my brother Tom, sister Peg and I had to go to Cowbridge to Miles the grocer to collect our groceries from his shop. This was next to where the Filco grocery shop is today. The grocery order would be given to the grocer the day before, and the three of us, loaded with shopping bags, or frails, would make our way home through Church Street and across the mill fields home to Llanblethian.

At Christmas my mother made a lot of cakes and tarts. She made eleven or twelve yeast loaf cakes. She wet the cake mixture, which consisted of flour, raisins, orange peel, yeast, and all other Christmas things, with a bottle of stout and we would each have a stir and a Christmas wish. We then had to fetch twelve tins from the bakehouse, the same tins that were used for baking the bread. Some cake dough was put into each tin. We then took them to the bakehouse for the baker to cook in his big oven alongside the bread. We would collect all the cakes the following day. The finished yeast cake was beautiful.

We nearly always had a lovely Christmas. There were never a lot of presents but we always received books.

As we grew older some of the household jobs were passed down from the older children to the younger. We had a bucket toilet at the top of the garden. It was the job of Tom and myself to dig a deep hole in the back garden every Saturday morning to bury the contents of the bucket. We had to scrub the toilet out with water, soap and disinfectant. We used a scrubbing brush and Jeyes fluid. We also had to clean out the chickens. We had about twelve and, when replacements were needed, we used to hatch our own eggs with the help of a broody hen. During the summer we had to weed the back garden path. Every Saturday morning it was the girls' job to help Mam scrub the flagstone floor in the kitchen and the flagstones to the front gate. When they were dry, sand was sprinkled on to the flagstones. After all the Saturday morning jobs were finished we were allowed out to play!

Every day, usually on the way home from school, we collected sticks for the fire from the fields. These would be put into the oven to dry for use the next morning. During the autumn, we gathered hazel nuts from the woods and blackberries for tarts from the hedgerows. My mother used to make elderberry wine. She also made carrot wine and beetroot wine and, during the spring, elderflower champagne. She also made nettle beer, which was known as herb beer. The elderberry wine was drunk warm for the treatment of colds in the winter.

★★★

My strongest lasting memory of my childhood days in the village is of long summer evenings. When I was very young I had to go to bed earlier than the older children, while it was still daylight. During those summer evenings the bridge over the river at the bottom of Broadway was a gathering place for older boys and girls. When I was reluctantly put to bed I could hear those young people on the bridge singing together like a choir. I can still hear the sound of those lovely voices mixed with the sound of sheep bleating and birds singing through the open window as I drifted off to sleep.

During the school holidays, we children were able to wander and walk anywhere we liked in the village and on Llanblethian Hill, and play Cowboys and Indians around and on top of the walls of St Quentin's Castle. There was never any worry about children being harmed anywhere. Our parents never even gave it a thought!

On fine days, we boys sometimes used to go up to Llandough Castle wood where there were plenty of rabbits. There was a high stone wall at the entrance to the wood pierced by a small hunting gate. We would pass through the gate and creep through the trees at the edge of the wood, where there was a long boundary fence which was full of rabbit burrows. We would always choose a fine, sunny day for these excursions. We would quietly arrange ourselves in a line along the bank between the burrows and the place where we thought the rabbits were sleeping. We couldn't see them, nor they us, although we could see the runs which went through the long grass. On a given signal we would all suddenly stand up clapping our hands and shouting. We could then hear the rabbits tearing through the long grass towards their burrows and us. As they broke cover to get to the safety of their hole they had to pass near to us. We always managed to catch a rabbit each, the number caught depending on the number of boys taking part. Not only was this wonderful fun but also the rabbit we each took home to our mothers was made into a delicious rabbit pie. As I usually accompanied my brother Tom on these trips our mother used to receive two rabbits!

Another popular outdoor activity was fishing. Mr Fred Evans, a retired tailor from Bridge House, Cowbridge, used to fly fish with rod and line. We spent many happy and interesting hours on the river with him. He fished the Thaw between Cowbridge, through Llanblethian, and down to about opposite the Lake Farm. He used to catch trout, which were plentiful in those days. There were also otters in the river then. He taught us how to catch trout by hand. We would lie on our tummies by the riverbank with our sleeves rolled up. Then we would slowly and quietly put our hand into the river and under the bank. This was the place where the trout usually lay quietly. Then we would, very gently, stroke the trout's tummy, slowly moving our hands towards its head where the gills were. As long as we kept stroking the trout they would not move. It was almost as if they had gone to sleep. Then we would grab them by the gills and throw them on to the bank. Some of the boys also fished under the big bridge by Greenfield. We would buy three little black fishing hooks from Williams the chemist in Cowbridge. Then we would cut a hazel or ash stick about one and a half inches across and two feet long. We split it at one end and would pass string through the split. We would tie a hook on the end of the string, and attach an earthworm to this. Then we would take off our stockings and, wearing an old pair of boots, would walk in the water under the bridge where we would slide the stick, hook and worm, in the water under the buttresses of the bridge. We never failed to catch eels there, which we would skin and take home. Mother would then fry them and they would make a good meal.

★★★

When I got older and my voice broke, I gave up the choir and took on the job of organ blower in the church. The pay for this was £2 a year, and I can remember that my first year's pay was put in a Post Office savings book. Also, when I was about sixteen years old I became one of the team of bell ringers in the church tower. There were six bells in the tower and I rang number five. My brother Tom rang number six, the harvest bell.

After church on Sunday mornings Tom, my sister Peg and I would walk over to the hunt stables where father was the main groom. There were about fifteen horses stabled there during the foxhunting season, and father would take us around to see them. He would get one out from its stall and give each of us a ride around the stable yard. The head groom was a Mr Chappell. He lived in the house and was in charge of five or six other young grooms who lived in the grooms' quarters. He was a strict, severe old man of whom we children were afraid. Mrs Chappell, his wife, was a really lovely lady. She always made a great fuss of us, giving us lovely cakes and sweets. I remember her very well.

Sir Sydney and Lady Byass owned Llandough Castle. I think that there were about forty outdoor and indoor staff employed there, including the grooms and three gamekeepers. The castle had its own cricket team, made up of members of the staff. They played on a well mowed and properly laid pitch near the hunt stables. On Saturday afternoons during the summer, one team would bat first then they would have tea before the other team had a turn at batting. Tom and I, together with a few other children, would always go to watch, and quite often we would keep score for them, using the makeshift score board. The tea was laid out on two long trestle tables by the stable. It was lovely food, cream cakes, and beautiful sandwiches, all from the castle. After tea, when the players were all back on the field, we would watch Mrs Chappell like hawks. When she raised her arm and beckoned to us we would all rush to her and sit down to eat what was left. We had such wonderful food there, things that we could never have at home. It was always a great day when the Llandough Castle cricket team played at home!

Llanblethian also had its own cricket and football teams. I played cricket quite often, on the Llandough Castle pitch. Our village team had a good record. At one time we went through two whole seasons without a defeat. The football team, which played in the Barry and District League, also did well.

Other village events included a flower and vegetable show each year. A big marquee was erected in Great House Field. As you walked through the entrance of the marquee there would be vases of sweet pea flowers being assessed by the judges. The wonderful perfume from the sweet peas would wash over you as you entered. It was unforgettable! After the judging was complete, there were the usual egg and spoon and sack races for the youngsters. It was always a wonderful day out.

Bonfire night was always celebrated on the top of Llanblethian Hill. We would all make our guys and carry them up the hill. Sometimes there would be as many as six or seven guys, a bonfire, and fireworks - a jolly evening indeed.

★★★

The village consisted mostly of small workingmen's cottages with only about three 'toff's' houses. They were the Cross, Stallcourt and Hill House and were all quite near to the church. By the river Thaw, there was a water mill, which was in full operation, a village shop, and a bakehouse, which baked the bread for the surrounding area.

We children used to stand by the door of the mill where the huge water wheel drove the millstones for the grinding of the grain, but we were never allowed inside because it was too dangerous. We used to watch the flour come down from the first floor, to chutes and then into bags. The local farmers went past our house, with their horses and carts, to take their grain to the mill for grinding. The Stone family ran the mill in those days. They had five children, three boys and two girls. Mrs Stone kept the shop in the mill house selling sweets as well as the myriad of things usually sold by village shops then. We used to spend our half penny or penny on sweets. The thing that I remember best about the shop is that they sold 'Dolly Mixtures' and we could buy a halfpenny's worth of them at a time. Mrs Stone weighed the sweets out on an old-fashioned balance with a brass bowl to hold the sweets. She kept the scales in the middle of the sweet jars, on a sort of platform, which raised them to almost eye level. This was so that she could make certain that, when she weighed the sweets, she never gave one too many. The Stone family was very industrious. Mrs Stone went to the market in Pontypridd once a week to sell her goods. The whole family used to gather mushrooms, blackberries, dewberries, and elderberries, all for sale in Pontypridd. She also sold her garden produce there. Many of the village women and farmers' wives did this as a way to make a little extra income. My family also grew vegetables. From when I was about seven years old I used to help in people's gardens bagging the potatoes and picking apples. I used to weed as well and usually I would be given a penny. The younger children would be lucky to receive a halfpenny.

The bakehouse was about fifty yards from the mill, and only about 100 yards from my home, in Greenfield Terrace. Johnny Thomas and his wife Jane usually baked the bread twice a week. We children always knew when Johnny was taking the tins out of the oven, using a long-handled wooden spade, because of the delicious smell of the freshly cooked bread. At those times we would all gather around the back of the bakehouse, where the oven stood, and stand just inside the door alongside the big wooden bin watching Jane tap the bread out of the hot tins with gloved hands. She would lay out the loaves on boards laid across the mixing bin, to cool ready for delivery the next day. When she turned out the bread lovely golden crumbs would fall off, and we children used to take turns to grab them and pop them in our mouths. They tasted wonderful!

The bread would be delivered the next day. Mr Thomas had an old-fashioned horse-drawn cart. His horse, Tommy, was kept in a field next to our house across Castle Hill. I can remember going to the field with Johnny the baker to catch Tommy, which was often difficult, but eventually we would harness him up to the covered cart and then load it up with loaves of bread for the delivery round. Johnny's delivery route would always start at the Cross Inn, then through Penllyn, Llansannor, Penylan, Newton, and finally to Aberthin. Johnny the baker would drive the horse and cart, and I would sit alongside him. We would set off at 10.00am and arrive back in Llanblethian at about 4.30pm with the bread all sold and delivered. Johnny used to stop at each pub in each village for a drink of beer while I waited outside in the cart. These pubs were the Cross Inn, Fox and Hounds, Barley Mow, City Inn, and finally the Hare and Hounds and Farmers' Arms in Aberthin. Needless to say, by the time we headed home from Aberthin, the baker would be quite drunk and I am sure that he sometimes dozed off to sleep between Aberthin and Llanblethian. Luckily Tommy knew the way home so that we always arrived back safely!

★★★

Winters were long, hard and very cold. Llanblethian was always flooded because of the river overflowing. All the meadows from the back of the High Street in Cowbridge through the village to Llandough Mill used to flood. I remember Llanblethian itself being covered with about twelve inches and more of water, from the bottom of the short steep hill in Piccadilly, along the road past the mill and the bakehouse, just up to our front gate in Greenfield Terrace. Also the road to the church schoolroom was covered in water.

Tramps used to come to the houses throughout the year to beg for food. Two tramps in particular used to come to our house. One of them was a man called Tom Milsom, and another was a very tall man whom we called Mr Big. They carried all their belongings on their backs. My mother used to give them bread, jam and cake as well as tea in their tin. They would sit outside the house on the small green at the bottom of Castle Hill to eat their food, and we children used to sit around and talk to them. They made interesting company and we were never afraid of them.

WALTER STONE, LLANBLETHIAN

Walter Stone, who still lives in Llanblethian near the mill, here describes the working of the mill up to its closure in 1948, and remembers the village as it was in his childhood in the 1920s and 1930s.

I was born in 1916; my father bought Llanblethian Mill in 1920. We came from Trerhyngyll; my father had a house there with a bit of land, but when the mill went up for sale he bought it, and ran it until 1948, when it was closed.

We were the last of the six mills which worked on the Thaw. Town Mill had gone by the time we came here, by 1918. By all accounts, Llewellyn Spencer was running the two mills, Town Mill and Llanblethian, and was renting Town Mill from the Williams family. He wanted a rent reduction but the Williams family wouldn't give it so he chucked it in and it went completely derelict. Only Llanblethian Mill was being worked by Llewellyn when he finished. Of the other mills, the farmer who had Gigman worked it a bit, but not on a commercial basis. When Tudor Llewellyn was in Howe Mill, there was no mill working. The old mill building was there, but I do not even remember a water wheel in it.

Ours was a breastshot mill – in fact all the mills on the Thaw were breastshot mills. There wasn't enough fall in the water for overshot mills, and the undershot were very inefficient. With the breastshot, the water came in half-way up the wheel into buckets on the wheel, and the weight of the water helped the wheel to turn.

Of course, the wheel wasn't working all the time. When the gate was down at the back of the mill, the water would pond back in the river as far as Town Mill, and then we'd let the water through to drive the wheel. In dry summers we'd have to wait for considerable periods until the water built up; that water we could use for an hour or so, but then the level would go down, and we'd have to stop the mill. We would then drop the gate down, and the river would eventually fill up to the top of the banks again. In very dry weather we could not get the amount of milling done, but on the whole we were not short of water. In fact, higher up, in the meadow, there was an overspill and after heavy rain, when the water rose so high, it would flow over into the Piccadilly brook.

There were two sets or pairs of stones – bigger mills had four or six sets. The bottom stone was stationary and the top stone revolved on top. The grain was fed through the centre of the stone. The stone was dressed, with veins in it which got thinner and thinner towards the end, and as the grain went in it got up these channels grinding all the time. As it came to the end it went into a wooden casing, and the wind and the force of the stone spinning worked the grain down to the chute which took the grain to the bottom storey of the mill. The stones were French burr, and they were set; some millstones were of solid stone, but others had the French burr set into plaster of Paris with a ring of steel on the outside; to turn one over to dress them you'd have to have a real good pulley, they were so heavy.

We dressed them with mill picks, made by a good blacksmith from very hard steel. When they wore down the smith pulled them out a bit further, he set them and ground them a bit and then he'd plunge them – but he had to know his colours because if you had a soft pick, it wouldn't last ten minutes. My father did most of the dressing himself. When we came here, there was an old millright, Old John we called him, he was a lovely chap. He taught my father – he said 'Harry I'm not going to last, am I?' – he was an old man then – he said, 'Harry, come and watch me do these stones'; and after a bit my father could dress the stones all right. Old John spent a lot of time here, part time, doing all sorts of things in the mill - such as fitting the wooden cogs. The drive to the mill was all of wood; in the big cast wheel there was a series of slots, and wooden cogs would be put in, shaped and pegged at the back. Old Gilead Spencer would make them for my father, and when they went in they'd drive in the edge they wanted to engage, and drive wedges down the back. I've fitted a good many of these cogs – sometimes you'd have a bit of a mishap and something would jam a bit and you'd strip a few cogs off. If you did this the stone wouldn't work, and then you'd have to go to old Gilead. My father always said that applewood was the best, but good old tough oak we used to get with Gilead, a knotted oak which had strength in it. Gilead was living next door but worked in the Bear Lane in Cowbridge. He and Harry Webb were the

Llanblethian Mill, with Harry, Connie and Walter Stone, 1927

wheelright and blacksmith there; they banded wheels together. Sometimes Harry Webb worked for my father as well if we had some metal break, he'd measure up and make the part. We all had to be prepared to repair things – I used to have to repair the buckets in the water wheel. Sometimes you'd lose a couple of them, perhaps the pegs that held them in would rot, and then you'd have a big area where the water would go straight through and you wouldn't have any strength there. If you lost two or three you'd be in trouble.

In the mill we ground up all sorts of grain – Plate maize or Indian Corn (from the river Plate in South America), Canadian wheat, and local wheat, barley and oats. All the oats and corn were for chicken or cattle feed. You could adjust the stones of the mill and sometimes my father would do kibbling - splitting the corn in half for chicken feed. Sometimes he'd grind it completely and it was like gold; the maize meal was beautiful, gold in colour: it fascinated me, like small gold floating down the chute. With oats the meal was a dull whiteish brown.

We could buy the foreign grain from Ranks in Barry, Pugsley and Wakelin on Cardiff docks, or Spiller and Baker (later Spillers) and my father had travellers from all those calling, and he gave big orders for wheat or corn. Sometimes he bought white flour from them as well. He bought grain in quantity, and he was pretty shrewd in his buying most of the time, though now and again he dropped a clanger - he bought high thinking the price would go higher, and it fell.

The grain would come in by wagon, in bags; there was a hoist in the mill, chain operated, and you could fix the bags on, push the chain against the wooden wheel and the chain would bite and up she'd go. It was using the power of the water, simple but very effective.

What we did as a rule was to take the grain in its raw state right up to the top floor, and it was laid out on the floor. They used to spread it into different areas and in the floor there were chutes, and you could feed that grain down into the hoppers to start the milling. They were canvas chutes – tied with a slip knot, so it could easily be directed into the hopper and down to the stones for grinding. We finished off at ground level – the meal or flour came down a fixed chute into a bin to be scooped out. Though it was possible to fill the bags straightaway, my father always ran it down into the built-in container areas. There was a wonderful machine for refining flour which had been built on the second floor, removing the bran with a series of sieves and brushes to make the pure white flour. Our bread made with that pure flour had a golden look on it.

Another thing my father did was to get the bakehouse going again. This was in the building over the river, where the bungalow Afon Ladrad is today. There was an oven there – it had gone into disuse and I don't think Llewellyn Spencer, our predecessor at the mill, had ever used it – it was a proper brick-built oven, which would take eighty to 100 loaves at a time.

We didn't bake for the village. Because the mill couldn't produce the quantity of flour we needed, we had to buy in flour as well but we made quite a bit of wholemeal flour, and made it into bread and sold it on our round. My father had started delivering with a horse and cart, but when he got going he bought a van. There were daily deliveries, to Llanblethian,

Walter Stone, about 1918

Cowbridge, Aberthin, Maendy, Trerhyngyll, Penllyn, City, Sigginstone, Llandough, and St Mary Church, six days a week. I took over the deliveries afterwards, and my father stayed here seeing to most of the bread making, though I was often up at 4 o'clock in the morning. We eked out a living, all of us – old Johnny Thomas near us was baking but he was only selling a small quantity, though he was going when we came to Llanblethian. There were five bakers coming round the villages – there was Gibbs in Cowbridge, Johnny Thomas and us, Tudor Liscombe from Llancarfan and then his chap started a round – he had the sack from Tudor and started a round. Today you can't get anybody to deliver.

We regularly supplied the Grammar School, which had quite a lot of boarders, and Dick Williams the headmaster once sent a boy over saying 'Tell Mr Stone to send some more bread'. Well, father said we'd have to get it done, but we were short of ordinary flour, Spillers or Ranks, so he used his own. He made big square 4lb loaves and sent them in. Mr Williams saw my father a few days later and played war with him. 'Mr Stone' he said, 'Don't you ever send us that bread again. I know what you've done'. 'I'm sorry, I was waiting for Ranks to deliver and so I had to use my own flour'. 'Well, don't you send it in here; those boys ate so much they will ruin us!' It showed the quality of our own flour; in commercial flour there's whitening stuff, but there were no additives in our flour made from Manitoba wheat, beautiful hard and dry wheat that the millers love.

We also supplied the High School, which also had some boarders, but only intermittently – it seems that the Co-op often managed to find out how much we had tendered for the contract and so often undercut us.

We closed the mill in 1948 after a visit from the River Board engineer and some local councillors. They explained that closing the mill gates was contributing to the problems of flooding upstream in Cowbridge, so we agreed to give up the water rights. By then we'd stopped making flour, and our main product was crushed maize and oats for cattle feed. But as more and more farmers were getting tractors, they could fix 'kibblers' to the tractors to crush the grain themselves, so it was about time to stop.

★★★

In Piccadilly, on the Llanblethian Hill side, there were in those days five cottages. After the Baptist Sunday School, the first two (today's Rose Cottage) were occupied by Darky Summers and the Chisells. Darky Summers was a Cornish bloke, he was a hell of a man. They reckon he used to get in trouble, he'd get boozed, and the cops couldn't hold him: he'd dart in between their legs. He moved over to the Bakehouse after a bit; in fact that first house changed hands a few times. The next two, now Half Moon Cottage, were where old Lil Jones and Mrs Boobyer lived, and then the last one (now Hill Drop) had a tin roof held on with wire and old Miss Williams lived there. There was one cottage on the other side where Roberts who did the murder on Llanblethian Hill in 1885 used to live; old Mrs Ridge lived there. She used to come home on Saturday nights with flagons in the pram, from Cowbridge. Old George Williams lived next door, in Brooklyn; he had a couple of fields and six or seven cows.

The kids used to play in the river – putting the worms with a hook on, under the walls, and pulling the eels out, sniggling they used to call it – you don't see any of it today. The sergeant was always asking 'Where's these boys of yours, Harry? I've had complaints.' 'Well, catch them' – 'But I can't catch them', he'd say to my father. Old Sgt Burston was always here about the boys, because we'd been putting taps on the windows and things like that. He was a good old sort. He'd have given us a row if he'd caught us, but he never caught us. We knew he was after us, and when we saw him we were gone.

There was no destruction, but the boys were up to everything. Girls, girls weren't safe: I can think of some who were beggars for the girls. Others, the younger ones, used to put taps on windows, a long ball of wool with a little washer on it, and they'd tap tap tap – and when someone came out they'd drop it, and of course in the dark no-one could see the wool or the washer. That's the sort of thing we'd get complaints about. The Girls' Friendly Society used to meet in the church hall, and what we'd do was bunk somebody up on the roof with a big clod of earth and a handful of grass. He would drop the grass down the chimney onto the fire, then stick the clod to block the chimney and smoke them out. Another thing we used to do – they used to make the tea outside and we'd go up and talk to old Baker or whoever was on there and we'd stick a couple of pounds of Epsom salts which we'd got from Williams the chemist into the tea water. It was harmless – no wilful destruction, but we used to play hell with the Girls' Friendly Society. It is a wonder that no-one was killed because we'd be up on the roof there – when you look at it today you'd wonder 'How on earth did we get up there?' We climbed everywhere, and almost lived on the castle walls – we would walk on the top of the castle walls and if any of us kids had gone over the top, that would have been it.

There were a couple of little shops in the village in the '20s – there was one up on Broadway, and my mother had one in the mill, selling bread and everything like that, and sweets. The only pub that was open was the Picton; I can remember old Tom Harkett coming up the Church Hill with a team of three horses for Hubert Thomas's father, from Penyrheol, Llysworney, and old Miss Llewellyn waiting for him at the top with a pint in her hand. That was service, that was.

ARTHUR JOHN, COWBRIDGE

Arthur John, the picture of whose mother and aunts appeared on the cover of *Cowbridge: Buildings and People*, here remembers Church Street in Cowbridge in the 1920s, and Y Bontfaen School in 1927. After a career in the army, Arthur lived in Cardiff until his death in September 2002, just after completing these reminiscences.

I was brought up by my grandparents, John and Miriam John, in 7 Church Street in Cowbridge. They both spoke Welsh, even though Miriam was from Bedford - she had learned the language after she had arrived in the Vale. Grandfather was noted for taking the role of the Mari Lwyd in its New Year procession through Cowbridge. He was known as 'Grassy' or 'Gras-y' as he had been brought up by his aunt Grace, in a cottage on the Aberthin road, next door to the Edmondes Arms in Cowbridge. He was noted for his interest in hunting, and was a terrier man for the Glamorgan Hunt. Having started with the hunt when he was fourteen, he worked for the hunt all his life, and was very popular with all the gentry. I remember the Mackintosh of Mackintosh, when on one of his visits to Cottrell, coming into the house to talk to him; Owen Williams of Crossways, too, visited us. Grandfather died in 1932 at the age of ninety-two. My brother Fred, a fireman, then took over the house.

Church Street as I remember it in the 1920s was quite different from the way it looks today. Where the Duke car park now stands were a shop and five houses. The first two houses, nearest to the High Street, were tall buildings, with a couple of steps up to the door; numbers 3, 4 and 5 were one-up, one-down cottages. None of them had any back garden to speak of, only space for the toilet and coalhouse - the coal had to be taken through the house.

On the corner with High Street was Thomas the saddler's shop, with harnesses hanging on the iron railings outside. That railing bar is still there.

Miriam and Johnny John (Arthur John's grandparents)
outside 7 Church Street

The house next door, No 1, was empty for some of the time when I was a child. I remember someone from Penylan living there, and then another couple, but the property was deteriorating. Next door lived the Carters, a large family. Charlie, Tom and Lewis all enlisted in the Welch Regiment. Tom went on to live in Rose Cottage, just outside the South Gate, and

Evan was a bellringer and father of Jack. 'Billo' David, a deliveryman for the Vale brewery, with three daughters, lived in No 3, then came the Rees family, Maud, Florrie, Lewis and Jack. Bert Cocks lived in No 5. He was a painter and decorator and he too had a large family, of seven children.

Next door to us lived Mrs Jenkins, Becky's grandmother. It was her responsibility to clean the church, from altar to the end. I used to help her from time to time - I would zoom with a duster up along the wooden seats, and back along the shelves. I was a member of the church choir, attending twice a Sunday, and going to the Sunday school in Cardiff Road as well. We didn't get paid for our attendance at choir, but I well remember receiving 2/6d, a lot of money in those days, for singing at the wedding of JC Clay and Mary Homfray.

Outside our house, cobbles stretching across Church Street marked the end of our property. There were iron brackets on the house wall, for lamps before the Gas Company started.

Opposite the Jenkins's house, on the other side of Church Street, was an old cottage, and between that and the church gate a narrow path led to the back of Arthur Mills's garage. He dealt in bikes as well as cars, and used to throw his scrap bikes out into the back lane. We boys used to cannibalise them for parts to make boneshakers with no tyres and no brakes. We used to have great fun using them on Constitution Hill - we would stop on the green at the edge of the road, or fall into the river!

The stables of the Duke were between the ballroom - where I remember the wind ventilator on the roof making a noisy clatter - and the back path. There were three boxes there and a tack room, where a groom slept. When the otterhounds used to come down from the Wye valley, they used the boxes to keep the hounds in. One day they would beat up river to City and back; the next day they would go down river to Aberthaw and back. In the yard next to the ballroom, Tom Pratt, the landlord, used to keep four pigs.

Going on through the South Gate, Rose Cottage was thatched, and was occupied by a railway guard, James John. Town Mill Road and the entry to the Poplars used to have massive elm trees along them. They had been cut down, and I remember the stumps were up to four feet across. The only buildings along Town Mill Road were Dynevor Cottage, then the Verlands and then Town Mill. The Sanders family lived in the left-hand house at the mill, and they had a little shop for sweets. John Sanders was a blacksmith, and had his forge in Eagle Lane.

Standard III in Y Bontfaen School, 1927

Back row: **Mr Billy Frederick**; **Arthur Jones**, West End Garage; **Ethel Smith**, from Primrose Hill, where the new cut joined the Roman road; **Carol Chisell**, Piccadilly, Llanblethian; **Peggy Jenkins**, Llanblethian (Bert's sister); **Phyllis Wilcox**, Aberthin; **Molly Wilde**, Llanblethian; **Joyce Deeves**, Westgate (her father sang alto in the choir); **Megan David**, daughter of Billy David the butcher; **Phyllis Trott**, who lived in a cottage at the end of Cooper's Lane; **Winnie Overton**, Westgate; **Gwyneira Llewellyn**, Llanblethian

Second row: **Arthur John**; **Jack Davies**, from a big house on the right hand side of the Limes; **Paddy McAdam**, son of Maths master at the Grammar School, lived in a bungalow opposite Cusop on Broadway; **Harold Oakley**, Croft Terrace, his grandfather Sam was a gravedigger; **Trevor Green**, Llanblethian; **Joe Cocks**, 5 Church Street; **Harold Tucker**, his family had shops where JBs is, and where the Bridge garage is today; **Malcolm Cooper**, Croft Street, china shop. Had earlier lived in Eastgate; **Walter Stone**, Llanblethian mill; **Ronald James**, Croft Street, father worked on the railway; **Mansel Thomas**, Aubrey Terrace

Front row: **Raymond Jenkins**, Llandough, father a groom with Sir Sydney Byass, Llandough Castle; **Marjorie Checkett**, father was a boot and shoe repairer, 24 High Street; **Charlie David**, lived in 3 Church Street with his grandparents; **John Harkett**, lived in a cottage on Broadway Hill in Llanblethian; **Bert Jenkins**, Llanblethian; **Colin Adams**, Bridge Farm, Llanblethian; later a pillar of Cowbridge Cricket Club; **Frank James**, Hillside, Llanblethian; **Glyn Spencer**, Brook House, Llanblethian; **Roy Cooper**, Malcolm's brother; **Herbert Janes**, The Kennels, Llanblethian; **Gwyneth Punter**, Croft Terrace; **Mr Sloman**, Headteacher

We used to cut across the fields from the mill to go to Bowman's Well for watercress, and then take a zig-zag path up Mount Ida, with the rocks called Devil's Foot and Knee half way up. We used to play in the castle, and would stage fights with bows and arrows, using willow branches for the bows, and reeds from the mill pond for arrows. We would also go skinny-dipping in the river, and then light a fire in the quarry across from the mill - where Mill Park is today.

We also used to go upstream of Cowbridge. There the Moors were very marshy: we would walk across them up to our knees in water. There was a lot of bird life among the reeds, and I remember corncrakes being common.

One particular character in Cowbridge was Jim Lewis the cooper, who lived opposite Old Hall. He was a very clever man, and I would stand for ages watching him make barrels. There was a real stink of glue in his living room, which was also his work room, full of his tools and stuff. He used to get the oak, cut it into slats, soak them, and put weights on them to get the shape of the barrel. He then took them outside and planed them to perfection. He would then put them in a metal band, with a sliver between them, put another band on, and put the shavings into the barrel and set fire to them. After cleaning that out, he would sandpaper all round, and put on another band to tighten them, using square nails, like studs. Before the top band was tightened, he would position the lid, which had a thin edge to fit in a recess he had planed at the top of the staves of the barrel. Jim Lewis was a real craftsman.

HERBERT DAVID, COWBRIDGE

Herbert David was born in Cowbridge in 1922, and worked in the family butcher's shop from the time of his leaving school until his war service in the RAF, and then until the shop closed in 1997. Here he deals with his family origins as well as his reminiscences about the family business to just after the end of the Second World War.

My mother's mother and her sisters were from west Wales, from Adpar in Cardiganshire. They came up here and worked for the Evans family, as housekeeper and cook and so on. Samuel David Evans had a draper's shop where Xantippe is today. It was a big old premises, bigger than it is today, because when Ivor Treharne bought it he knocked a lot of it down. In the back of that the Evanses had built what the locals called the 'American flats' to house staff. They had tailors, seamstresses, dressmakers, milliners. If you

Herbert David in the office of the shop at 36 Eastgate, 1996

76

wanted a man's suit in those days, there was only one place you would go in the Vale of Glamorgan - that was Evans of Cowbridge. They'd make it there. They got nearly all their staff from down west, and that's how my grandmother came to Cowbridge.

My grandfather on my mother's side was a shoemaker. They lived in Eastgate, and he was on the local council - Isaac Thomas. They had about nine children, and were Welsh speaking. The school headmaster used to send my grandmother, Ruth, a note, saying, 'Stop speaking Welsh to the kids. I can't get the lessons across to them.'

My father's family were from Miskin, near Pontyclun. When my father's father married, he went to live in Pendoylan. I don't know what he did for a living but, when my father was very small, he moved to Cowbridge. They'd started building the Aberthaw line, and there was tremendous work going on. There was a very deep cutting to start with. It was a lovely line, lovely scenery - it went through Beaupre great park - but it never paid.

My father, William David, learned his trade with a butcher in Cowbridge, by the name of Thomas. He left school at fourteen, as did my mother. They were apprenticed to a trade in those days. That's gone now. But if I'd had sons, I wouldn't have expected them to have carried on. The work is too hard. In those days, the local authority would give the master butcher about £25 for taking on an apprentice.

My mother was apprenticed to Mrs Miles, a solicitor's wife, who used to do some sewing 'on the side', but she must have been recognised as a good tradesperson. Where Jenny Wren is now, there was a big old property, Taynton House, where the solicitor's office was. Mrs Miles lived there right up until she died - I think she died during the last war. My mother remained friendly with her, but never took on the sewing business because she married and had four children, and she helped in the butcher's shop. Sometimes my father would leave her to it when he went off to market, and she enjoyed it. Just like a farmer's wife, she was expected to do her share. She might have cut a little bit of meat, but she was no expert at it.

My parents must have got married about 1912. Whether he saw it advertised in the paper or whether it was word of mouth I don't know, but my father bought a small butchery business in Hayes in Middlesex. They lived there for two years, but he was the right age to be called up for the army, and he had to leave the business. He trained for about three or four months, went out to France, and got wounded in Passchendaele in Belgium. He was shipped back to this country with shrapnel wounds in the back, lost a lung - a very big thing in those days - and was in hospital for two years. The medical people told him he wouldn't be able to do any heavy work.

My father was discharged from the forces, because of his wounds, on a fifty-per-cent pension. Back in Cowbridge, his wife, my mother, was living with her mother in 37 Eastgate Street. It was near the station entrance. There was the Druids Hotel, then the road going to the railway yards, then the old ticket office on to the road, then the road to the new station built for the line to Aberthaw. Next, there's a house which is called Glen Cottage, and a very small house next to it, 37 Eastgate. Being an old house, whoever lived there built on out the back, so it was larger than it looked. That was where my grandfather had his shoe shop. He married the Evanses' cook, and she opened a shop in the front and sold bread and cakes. It was called Adpar House.

My father used to come home from hospital in Windsor. He was walking down the street one day in about 1917, in his 'army blue' (wounded soldier's uniform), past the butcher's shop where Eastgate Gallery is now. Thomas the butcher came out and said, 'Look here, Billy. My wife has left, and I want you to take over the business.' He said to my mother, 'We'll move into this big old house behind the shop'. They went to see it and it was in a hell of a state, and my mother said, 'I'm not moving in there.' There was a small shop next door to the Commercial Hotel, owned by a chap by the name of Williams, living in Cardiff Road, and my father asked to rent the shop. The house was in a pretty good state, so my father finished down in Thomas's, and opened the other shop. We kids were born there, at 26 Eastgate. It was known as Bristol House, and was right opposite the station. It was a good position, because miners used to come down on the train from the valleys and go on the booze in Cowbridge, and decide to take a good leg of Welsh lamb back with them.

They settled in that house, then the Edmondes people in Old Hall wanted to sell up. They sold a good few houses in Cowbridge, but I think they only owned one field. My father bought that four-acre field, Cae Stumpie, in 1922 for £300. Butchering and farming went together, so he kept some stock in the field, and he got Bob Thomas the builder to build him a slaughterhouse there. That was Bob Thomas's first big job. You didn't have to have permission in those days; you just built it. My father

WJ David, evacuee and pigs in the 'Stumpy Field', 1940s

didn't have much experience of buying livestock, but he soon picked that up. He was shrewd as far as money was concerned.

There were lots of markets in those days – not only a market in Cowbridge, but also in Ystradowen, Wenvoe, Bridgend and Llantwit Major. He didn't go to them all. He'd go mainly to Cowbridge market and buy a couple of pens of lambs (about twelve lambs) and a bullock. He'd produce his own pork, because he was keeping pigs by the slaughterhouse. If we bought a bullock in the market, we had to drive it down the street. One day, one ran into Arthur Sanders's shoe shop and couldn't back out, so we had to drive him round the kitchen table to turn him round and get him out again. I'm glad to say he didn't make a mess in there.

Before the war, we rented a couple of other fields around the town - on the Cardiff and St Athan roads - where we ran about thirty to forty ewes, producing our own lamb. We used to buy a couple of store cattle every year, and we had a 'house cow' - for milk. I don't know what breed they were. A chap by the name of Thomas, who built a house in Llanblethian just before the war, used to farm about 300 acres near Boverton, and the government took it over in the 1930s because times were bad. They brought people down from the Rhondda hoping to get the miners to run smallholdings at Trebeferad and New Barn. They gave the families a house, a couple of acres and a cow. Many never made a go of it. Then they started building RAF St Athan, the cows were sold and the men went to work on the 'drome. That could have been where our cow came from.

Initially meat was kept in ice boxes - you could buy ice and have it sent to Cowbridge in sacks from the cold stores in Cardiff docks. My father bought his first fridge, which was a Frigidaire, in Cowbridge Show in about 1930. I can remember it. My father was the type of man who didn't drink a lot, but went out nearly every night of the week, had a couple of halves of beer, and that was it. He would talk to people. We supplied the Williamses in the Bear for donkeys' years, an order in those days of at least £200 a week. We also supplied the Duke - old Tom Pratt kept it, a good customer again. The Frigidaire man came down to stay in the Bear for a couple of days. Talking to my father in the bar, he asked my father for a good lamb to hang in the fridge on show day, and said he could put his name on it for free advertising. My father bought the fridge off the showground, because it was offered to him £20 cheaper. It would have cost about £300, a lot of money - the same as he paid for the field, and the same as it cost to build the slaughterhouse. You can hardly believe it.

'Tom the Horse' used to deliver meat for us, and the horse was also used for haymaking and so on. Later, we delivered by car (after 1928) or bike. Before the war, most meat was delivered. By the 1930s, we were all working in the business. In 1935, my father bought Rhoscelyn in 36 Eastgate, and that became our family home and shop. My brother Edward and I started working in the shop when we were fourteen, but I could dress a lamb when I was twelve years old. My father taught me at the same time as he taught my brother. He thought that it was the best thing for us, to come into the business.

We saw some good times; but then came rationing, when things were controlled by the Ministry of Food. It started almost straight away, almost as soon as war started. By 1940, there were lots of controls. My brother was the right age to be called up for the first militia men, so he volunteered and joined the RAF. He went to Italy and north Africa. I was in the Home Guard before I joined the RAF. I served about four and a half years. All that time, my father managed on his own, with help from my mother and my eldest sister. There was nobody else. With rationing, the shop lost a lot of trade. Some weeks, my father was only having £20 worth of meat (at wholesale price) to make a living on. It was supplied from a big slaughterhouse in Barry. Our slaughterhouse was empty. My father could have kept the pigs, but he had too much to do with the shop.

The Pavilion cinema in Eastgate went back right up to the fence of our field. It had a lovely ballroom and dining room. Metro Goldwyn Mayer had a distribution centre in Cardiff, but moved it out to Cowbridge because of the fear of air raids. The owner rented them the ballroom as offices. MGM were there for about eighteen months, and rented the slaughterhouse for a store room and distribution centre for all the cans of film. The bloomin' cinema caught on fire and was burned to the ground. There was not much bombing in Cardiff after all. After that, the slaughterhouse stayed empty, and never reopened.

After the war, my father let the Cae Stumpie Field, with the slaughterhouse, go to the Council for council houses to be built. It was the only land left in the town. This is where Borough Close is today.

After the RAF, I went straight home, and my brother went to work in Cardiff, but eventually he came back to the business. The rationing went on so long, till about 1953. There wasn't much black market activity. I don't think sausages were rationed, but the butcher might make 100lbs of sausages if he had a bit of spare meat, and he could offer them to customers who came in. We used to make a lot of sausages. We didn't have time to make a variety, because we were tied to traditional ways of doing things. We had good rounds to farms and I started a good delivery round on the RAF camp in St Athan. My brother came home to stay because I was ill, packed in his job in Cardiff, and he took over the round. My father was getting on, but he never finished altogether, because he and my mother lived behind the shop until they died in the mid-1970s. He used to stick his nose around the door to see how we were doing.

ALF CHARLES, TRERHYNGYLL, MAENDY AND YSTRADOWEN

Alf Charles, now a long-time resident of Cowbridge, here remembers his childhood in Trerhyngyll and New Forest near Ystradowen in the 1930s and early 1940s.

I was born in 1927, and lived in Trerhyngyll for most of my early life, until we moved to New Forest, west of Ystradowen, in 1932-3. One of my earliest memories is going to the March Fair in Cowbridge. My grandfather, with whom I lived, had a tradition of sowing his onion seeds on March Fair morning (weather permitting), and then we would go by train to the fair which used to fill the Bear Field. There were swing boats, test-your-strength machines, dodgem cars, and many other attractions including Scarrott's boxing booths. I hated those but my brother always wanted to watch the boxing. There would be someone outside the booth challenging all comers to fight his man, who was usually standing alongside him. Young fellows who fancied their chances, and in the hope of winning a pound or two, would go into the ring and get battered. Those were the days when Tommy Farr was still fighting in the booths. By contrast, one of the things children used to love to buy were straw balls, wrapped in silver paper, and on a length of elastic; with these there would be mock battles with friends.

My grandmother had worked at Great Frampton Farm when she was a girl, towards the end of the nineteenth century - for her keep and £3 a year. She used to tell us that she would save a few shillings to spend in the March Fair - this was their one outing of the year. She also said that one year when she came to the fair, a gale sprang up and the many stalls which lined the High Street near Woodstock House were blown over, and their wares scattered along the street.

In Trerhyngyll, I lived in Rose Glen, on the left opposite Lilac Cottage. In those days Trerhyngyll was divided into two distinct parts, with a 'green belt' between them. You lived either in 'Top Trerhyngyll' or 'Bottom Trerhyngyll' - these parts are now linked by new development. At the appropriate time of the year, pigs were killed on a wooden bench on the grass verge in front of Rose Glen. My grandfather kept his pigs in the adjoining pigsty. My grandmother was a great maker of black puddings - using the blood and innards of the pig, onions and flour. Home-made faggots, too, were always very tasty.

There was a duck pond in Trerhyngyll, now a lovely lawn, but you can still see irises growing in the stream which flowed into the pond. Ducks and geese used to waddle up and down the road and the men in the village would clear out the pond every now and then for the ducks. There were two well-greens in the village, one in the top village where there is now a playground, the other in the bottom village (now part of a garden). Mr and Mrs Radcliffe, of Green Farm, kept a lot of turkeys coming up to Christmas - these used to wander onto the road and frighten us children as they were very big birds. My aunt lived in the Malsters, formerly a pub with its own brewery, and we often enjoyed playing in the ruins of the malthouse.

Romany gypsies were regular visitors to Heol-y-Bant in Trerhyngyll. They were very clean, and the only sign of their stay was a little circle of ashes where they had their camp fire. They had very colourful horse-drawn caravans, with their saucepans and frying pans hanging on hooks under the van. We children were a little afraid of them, but the adults got on well with them.

A memorable event was St Mary Hill Fair, in August, towards the end of the forty days of St Swithin. Grandfather would gather together a little group of us children and walk us from near Ystradowen (we had moved to live in New Forest by then) to the fair, a long, exhausting walk in the heat of the day. Here there were beer tents, cheap jacks, stalls, and of course horse sales. It was a great attraction for travellers and gypsies. We had to watch our step on the fairground because all around us there would be people trying out the horses, cantering and galloping. Fights would break out, probably as a result of too much drink, and the combatants would go down to a corner of the field where they could fight undisturbed. I remember on one occasion one fellow took on two or three others at the

Mrs Radcliffe with milk separator, Green Farm, Trerhyngyll

same time, while in the distance a couple of bobbies were walking up and down, seemingly paying no attention at all.

My grandparents' house was out in the country, but we had some regular callers including the packman, carrying a suitcase of clothes, cottons and needles for sale. He came on foot, and would carry on across the fields to Llansannor. Another man, Mr David of Tongwynlais, came in his Austin 7 with an assortment of clothes. He would arrive on a Friday morning, usually once a fortnight, and in the holidays we would wait for him to give us a lift to the Ystradowen village shop. I remember that Mr David very kindly offered to go to Evan Roberts of Kingsway, Cardiff, to buy my first Grammar School cap. The cap was essential in those days - woe betide you if you were not wearing your cap - but Cardiff was a long way by bus or train.

One day, on our way to school, my brother and I met a tinker's cart, two-wheeled and horse-drawn, festooned with pots and pans and baths for sale, on its way to Llanharry.

Other regular annual visitors to the area were the onion sellers from Brittany (known as 'Shwni-onion men') with strings of onions hanging from the handlebars of their bikes. My grandfather would offer to sell them some as he always had plenty of onions hanging in the garden shed. I was always surprised that these men found their way to such lonely places in the hope of making a few pence profit.

We had twice-weekly visits from two bakers and confectioners - Bartletts of Pontyclun and Retters of Talbot Green. Mr Retter, who always wore highly polished leggings, carried a chest of shallow drawers in his van containing a variety of delicious cakes. He would open these drawers in turn, so that we could choose a cake if we had a penny or halfpenny to spare. Another caller on a regular basis was a man (from Llanharan I think) on a grocery bicycle with a deep carrier on the front, laden with groceries for sale. My grandmother would buy a jar of lemon curd just to help his sales, as she got most groceries from Bartletts or Retters.

Mr Bartlett, the baker, would take our accumulators (for running the Marconi radio) for recharging, and bring them back on his next visit. If there was no spare charged accumulator, we had to manage without radio for a few days; the radio also needed a large dry battery, and there were frustrating times when this ran down. Coal merchants and hardware sellers also called, the latter carrying paraffin in a large tank in the back of the van. This was essential for the oil lamps.

Like many other people in isolated areas, we had to carry drinking water from a well; this was a good half mile from the house and it was hard work carrying the water in pitchers or jacks, sometimes during pouring rain. In times of drought, the tanks at home would dry out and extra water would have to be carried from the well.

During the war, we would help in the hay and corn fields, such was the demand to produce more and more food. There was little machinery - only horse-drawn rakes and swathe turners - so much had to be done by hand. There was double summer time, the clocks being put forward two hours to make longer light evenings. In school holidays and at weekends we would stay on the fields until after midnight, cocking hay, stooking corn, or helping to collect the hay or corn.

When my grandfather was still well enough, he would order chicks, a few days old, from breeders in other parts of the country. Mr Lewis, the Ystradowen stationmaster, would send someone to say that they had arrived, and my grandfather, brother and I would go along as soon as possible to collect the chicks, twittering away in their cardboard box. Grandfather also regularly ordered his seed potatoes from Perth in Scotland;

these also came by train, but it was not quite so urgent to collect them. Another regular trip with my grandfather was to the Llanharry limekilns to collect lime for the garden or for decorating the cottage walls.

For us, Ystradowen was the centre of our activities. The vicar was Revd JC Payne, a good Christian with great concern for his people in those very difficult times when there was no welfare state. On the days of the Sunday school outings - by bus to Porthcawl or Barry in alternate years - he would insist that we went into church before leaving, to pray for a fine day. Our prayers were usually successful, as I remember only one occasion when it poured with rain all day, and we spent the whole day in the shelter on the promenade at Barry Island. On some Sunday evenings during holidays, Revd Payne would say to us choirboys 'You boys come down to the vicarage tomorrow at one o'clock'. We would learn next morning that his son, Mervyn, had been seen leaving the village shop with bottles of lemonade, and on arrival at the vicarage we all - six choirboys, the vicar and his wife - were jammed into the car, and we drove off to the beach at Llantwit Major for the afternoon. We were also taken to the Leys, and on one occasion to Aberavon. There were annual fetes on the vicarage lawn, and these were always well attended; the 'fortune teller' who operated in the garage would cause much hilarity amongst the adults.

Another social centre of the village was the old church hall, between the vicarage and the railway bridge, and very similar to the one which still exists in City: asbestos walls and timber lined. There was a little stove to heat it, and oil lamps hanging from the ceiling. Here we used to go to the weekly 'Penny Readings'. We paid a penny admission fee, and most of us were expected to recite or sing. It was a kind of 'go as you please' and made for an entertaining evening. We also saw some good drama productions here. The vicar's brother ran an amateur dramatics group in the Rhondda, and once or twice a year he would bring them down to perform a play, like 'Maria Martin and the Red Barn'.

It was in this hall, on a brilliant moonlit night in January 1941, that we had a Sunday school concert. Soon after the start, the Luftwaffe launched a heavy attack on Cardiff. Even at twelve or thirteen miles distance, the hall seemed to shake as the bombs fell and anti-aircraft guns responded. I was taking part in a sketch, forgot my lines, and the sketch ended in about half its allotted time. As we walked home afterwards, we looked towards Cardiff to see the explosion of bombs and ack-ack shells, with searchlights criss-crossing the sky.

Church Farm, Ystradowen

The hall was the centre for the distribution of gas masks in 1939, and for their upgrading when an extra filter was attached with green tape. It was also the HQ for the village troop of the Home Guard.

At this time, there were only about fifteen houses in Ystradowen. The vicarage was really out of the village, beyond the railway bridge on the Cowbridge road. After the bridge, Church Farm still stands on the left; opposite Church Farm and behind the sawmills yard was the stationmaster's house, a very nice house. It was sad to see it decay for many years after the railway line fell out of use. The sawmills were owned by a Mr Edwards of Coity, and managed by Mr Charles Morris. The mills were always busy at that time; the saws were operated by a steam engine. Mr Arthur Jones, undertaker and carpenter, had his workshop in a small part of the sawmills yard – we used to go and watch him making coffins. He subsequently moved his business to JB Builders Merchants in Cowbridge. His descendants still run that business.

After Church Farm came the White Lion, tenanted for many years by Mr and Mrs Tom Russell. There, against the church wall, was a hand-operated petrol pump. Then came Ty Mawr. It was a shame that this building, which must have been fine in its heyday, was ever demolished. It had a large farmyard, a big pond in front of it and a well, reached down some steps, adjacent to the road. Next were the three 'poor houses' on the corner of the Welsh St Donats road, where there is now a green with a letter box. There were two large ones and the third was quite tiny. They had corrugated roofs, and were probably thatched under that. The fronts faced away from the main road towards the south and the sun. Opposite these cottages, Ty Melyn, where two elderly spinsters lived (Ruth Willis and Jane John, aunt and niece), was followed by the three cottages of Park Terrace (across the present entrance to Ash Grove) with very large gardens behind. Phyllis Miles lived in one of the cottages. I remember her stopping us on our way home from church on the morning of September 3rd, 1939, to tell us that war had been declared. Her grandmother lived in another cottage; she had been bedridden for years, but still organised the village and district newspaper distribution from her bed.

Next to Park Terrace came the shop, in the house now known as Ty Mawrth. The shop was in a small front room, and customers had to go through the living room to reach it. Mr and Mrs Gibbon, the elderly couple who kept it, were Welsh speakers - he was born and brought up in Ystradowen, she was from Pontyclun. She was a stout lady who was unable to move much, and would sit sideways on to the table in the living room, facing the door. Her husband would accompany you into the shop. Once I wanted writing paper and as he was a bit deaf he turned to his wife to ask what I wanted. 'Papur ysgrifennu' came the reply, and he then understood.

Past Ty Mawrth on the lane up towards Ash Hall was a small cottage with a blacksmith's shop attached. On our way home from school, we would have a go at pumping the bellows while the smith was shoeing horses or making iron rims for cart wheels. Just opposite the entrance was a little stream which he would block off to make a small pond where he would dunk his hot irons to cool them. Back on the main road, next came the old Tudor Arms where Tom Griffiths the blacksmith lived - he was uncle to Don and Roy Griffiths of Cowbridge. Finally, there was one smaller cottage below that (Mrs Wareham's). From this point in particular one could see the Ystradowen moors, sometimes on fire, the grass having been set alight by the sparks from the train. The fires were spectacular but I cannot remember whether anyone came to put them out or whether they were just left to burn themselves out.

The Silver Jubilee celebrations in 1935 were held in Maendy in the field opposite the Manse, which was the house on the bank on the east side of the road between Maendy and Ystradowen. The field was used for football - Maendy had a very good football team, and played practically every Saturday. The team really consisted of people from the catchment area of Maendy school: one of the stars was Mervyn Evans of Aberthin (and later of Cowbridge).

The Manse was the home of Revd TT Jones, minister of the Congregational chapel in Maendy, and another excellent Christian. We were fortunate to have two such ministers of religion to look after us. Revd Jones was the minister at Maendy for fifty-four years, 1890 to 1944. The chapel was usually full, and the services were in Welsh. He lived first in Trerhyngyll until the Manse was built for him. He was a north Walian, and when he came to Ystradowen church - as he did from time to time - took ages to read the lesson in English. He was always much happier speaking in Welsh. He was succeeded by the Revd Jeremiah, also Welsh speaking, who ran a Young People's Guild, held in the chapel vestry every Thursday evening. We had very pleasant times there, and it was well attended, even by young men who had returned from war service.

In Maendy, there was Maendy Isha, then the four cottages of Maendy Ganol, Maendy Uchaf Farm, Red House (the post office) opposite, then the house later occupied by Miss Dena Williams, headmistress of Y Bontfaen School. On the other side of the Cowbridge road and along the road to Prisk was the headmaster's house, next to the school. Near it was Maendy House owned by Mr Bryn Edwards (then French master at the Grammar School). Opposite was Pwll Du, then occupied by Brent Busby's grandparents. Old 'Maen Dy' where Mr Williams lived was a stone cottage in front of the school, and must have given its name to the village. It was demolished while I was still at Maendy school, and was replaced by the school shrubbery.

There was a good bus service through Ystradowen and Maendy, a double decker operated by the Rhondda Transport Company. The buses ran every hour from Talbot Green to Cowbridge but, during the summer, there was a half-hourly service, with every other bus going on to Barry Island. There was also a good train service from Llantrisant to Cowbridge. Before and during the war there was an autocar service (push-pull) so that only the driver had to change places at Cowbridge. Another type of engine was the tank-type, which had to be shunted in Cowbridge and put on the front of the train for the return journey. I travelled to Cowbridge Grammar School daily on the train. The autocar was divided into two, girls one side, boys the other, with a small entrance passage in between where the guard sat. Sometimes the train would have separate compartments, and I am told that some of the more daring boys would climb out of one compartment into the next as the train crossed the Ystradowen moors.

Returning from school on Monday afternoons we would usually see soapsuds running down the cobbled gutters of Eastgate, Monday being the recognised washday. There were two wide entrances to the railway property – the one next to the Druids led to the goods yard, and to the right, next to Glen Cottage, was the entrance for passengers. The old ticket office separated the two approaches. We would rush up to the platform, where the guard would always chivvy us: 'Hurry up or we'll miss the London', because it was a connecting train to the London line at Llantrisant. During the war, large quantities of timber were stacked in the goods yard for seasoning – we assumed it had come from Cardiff or Barry Docks to escape damage by enemy action.

On one occasion during the war, the train did not run because incendiary bombs had been dropped in the vicinity of the Cowbridge signal box. A Western Welsh bus was substituted for the train, and ran through Ystradowen via the Ash Hall road to Llanharry and Llantrisant, with the train guard acting as conductor. This pleased me as I was dropped off much nearer my home than the railway station.

I left the Grammar School at fifteen, having taken my physics exam in July 1942 on my fifteenth birthday. John Dale Owen, the acting headmaster, told us that if we didn't have an exam in the afternoon we should go home and get some sleep before the German bombers came over. They had a peculiar throbbing engine noise, quite unlike our own planes, and it was quite frightening to hear them. I then went on to Bloggs College in Cardiff, opposite the New Theatre, for a short time to study shorthand and book-keeping. I used to go by train from Ystradowen, changing at Llantrisant; then the main line train stopped at Peterston, St Fagans and Ely, before getting to Cardiff.

ELGIVA THOMAS,
COWBRIDGE GIRLS' HIGH SCHOOL

Elgiva, whose husband Alan (pictured with her) has also contributed to this collection, here gives her memories of Cowbridge Girls' High School in the 1930s, when she lived in St Hilary. She still lives in the village today.

I attended Cowbridge Girls' High School in the 1930s. There were boarders as well as day girls, with the boarders sleeping in the 'upstairs section' next to the matron's room. The headmistress had her office and sitting room downstairs.

Our headmistress, Miss Bennett Jones, 'Benny', was quite unusual. She kept a pet monkey, which wore a little jacket and hat, made - as rumour would have it - by the girls who did needlework. The monkey was allowed to roam everywhere, and spent quite a lot of time in the boarders' dining room, where the day girls had lunch. Once I was standing near a radiator in the room. I had been give a pen and pencil set for my birthday, and had the pen clipped on to my gymslip. The monkey, on the window, pinched my pen from my gymslip and climbed up on to the window again, so I went into my form room, got the board pointer, and tried to use it to dislodge the monkey so that I could get my pen. The monkey slid down the pointer and bit my hand; the bite in time went septic. My parents protested and so Benny got rid of the monkey. It is said that she took it to Bristol Zoo; some of the more malicious girls suggested that she went to visit it once a fortnight.

Cowbridge High School for Girls, Form Va, 1935

Back row: Nina David, Lillian Deveril, Rhoda Greening, Bex Rees, Miss Maud Gunter,
Lucy Hopkins, Eirwen John, Marion Isaac, Isabel Barrie, Nancy Blanch
Middle row: Dinah Harding, Evelyn Hill, Catherine Radcliffe, Mavis Hill, Eileen Hyde,
Peggy Williams, Elizabeth Gronow, Edna Lewis
Bottom row: Bronwen Treharne, Elgiva Young, Gwen James, Kathleen Wiggins,
Doreen Parsons

Benny cycled to Maendy chapel regularly, and – another eccentricity – used to take her bicycle into one of the pews in case anyone stole it. Benny's sister was a Mrs Crystal, the proprietress of a tearoom called the Copper Kettle in the Castle Arcade, Cardiff. Whenever there was any form outing to the theatre we were compelled to have tea in the Copper Kettle – always 'sawdust cake', bread with a semblance of a scrape of margarine, no jam, and weak tea. For this, in 1931-2, we were expected to pay two shillings. 'Whatever are you having, for that amount of money?' my mother asked. 'Is it for one, or for the whole form?'

One day, Benny decided the school was to have a radiogram. We all had to contribute 2/6d, a considerable sum in those days, and I can remember only two occasions when we were allowed to listen to it. The biggest girls in my form had to push it into the hall from the headmistress's office - and we heard Lewis Casson and Sybil Thorndike reciting a scene from Macbeth and, by contrast, Paul Robeson singing 'Go and ring dem bells'.

When I started school, the uniform for junior girls was blouses and gymslips, with skirts for the senior girls, but it soon changed to blue and white gingham dresses with white cuffs and collars. In summer we had speckled straw hats and, later, panamas with the school hatband. We also had to wear burberry coats, with scarves and gloves in winter. If for any reason we went into town - such as to the Bear Field to play hockey, or when the boarders went to tea on Sundays to Nurse Rymer's café - we always walked in crocodile, and always wore gloves. The boarders had a grey uniform.

I took school lunch with the boarders when I started school, but I could not tolerate it, so then I ate my sandwiches in the kitchen. Benny would come around with a board pointer to check if we were sitting upright - if not, she would poke us firmly in the back with the pointer. She made sure of our table manners - and if a girl held her knife as if it were a pen, she would ask 'Are you signing your name on your meat?'

During the whole time I was in school, the most severe punishment possible was a conduct mark. I never remember anybody getting one, but order marks flew about, especially from Miss Marks, the Maths teacher. She would bite and push out her lower lip when she became enraged. Miss Williams, English, was very severe and had no sense of humour. She wore big owl-like spectacles. Miss Gunter was very erudite about Cowbridge. She was so enamoured of the geography of Cowbridge that she used to claim that there were more meanders in the river Thaw than in the Mississippi, and we got the impression that Mount Ida was higher than Kanchenjunga! She taught History very well, and made people interested, but in the first form Benny taught us and it was she who fired my imagination. She was a very good teacher.

May Brown had a good sense of humour. She never became really cross, and could laugh things off. She taught Welsh, Latin in the first form, and Music. She was lovely, and had no favourites - she was very pleasant, and the same to everybody. Miss Powell who taught Latin was in digs with my aunt and uncle next door to the Railway Inn (in part of Basil's today). We got on well with her; she treated us as equals. Miss Morgan, teacher of cookery and needlework, also had a mature attitude. When the girls who did cookery had finished the morning's cooking, the boarders would rush to the door to ask if there were any left-overs. Burnt or uncooked, they would be scoffed down by the boarders. That room had coal-fired ovens; sometimes it was so hot you could hardly enter the room.

Mrs Phillips the gym teacher was about seven feet high, with junoesque legs like tree trunks. I was no good at gym - I could never jump over the horse. Soon afterwards, Mrs Phillips was replaced by Miss Phillips who was physically the complete opposite - string thin, quite small, with a very loud voice and commanding personality.

Finally, the peripatetic music and singing teacher, Miss Miles. She came to us twice a week - I don't know if she was able to go elsewhere after taking us! She was meek and timid, the last thing you want with schoolgirls. I am ashamed to think that we gave her a terrible time: we would sing the wrong tune to the words or the wrong words to the tune, and she would go red in the face.

At break times, we would walk round the tennis courts and along around the perimeter of the school, perhaps more than once. In our final year we were able to sit on the wrought iron seats near the tennis courts, and I remember the power of telling any juniors who were sitting there to move off!

Looking back, I enjoyed my schooldays. I was very happy at Cowbridge High School.

ALAN THOMAS,
LLYSWORNEY AND COWBRIDGE

Alan Thomas, husband of Elgiva and brother of Hubert, here recalls his early days in Llysworney mainly in the 1930s, and at Cowbridge Grammar School at the end of that decade and in the early years of the war. After a career as a chartered quantity surveyor, he now lives in retirement at St Hilary.

I was born in Great House, Llanblethian, but we moved to Penyrheol Farm, Llysworney - the farm of my mother's family - when I was four years old. I went to the village school in Llysworney, where we had a very dedicated schoolmistress, Miss Grant. It was such a small school that there was only one other teacher. Miss Grant was a disciplinarian - she could cane like nobody's business, on the hands only - but she was ahead of her time in getting us aware of our environment and in organising outings. On half days - given for good attendance or some such reason - we would go to the local beaches where she would get us to play cricket, and she would play, too, even though she had some problems with her leg. At least once a year she would get the 'Wick charabanc' from Mr Williams of Wick, to take us on outings to Bristol Zoo or other far away places. She also helped organise the village Christmas party, always a memorable occasion.

One particular village event which I remember was the Silver Jubilee celebrations for King George V in 1935. The function was held in Nash Manor. There was dancing around the maypole, and I was chosen to propose the toast to the King and Queen. It was a great carnival; I was dressed as an Arab sheikh - Hubert helped me dress up - and all the village took part.

Llysworney Show was another big event of the year. It was a very successful little show, mainly horticultural, with marquees for flowers and for vegetables, and other tents too. There were also horse riding and jumping competitions, and a brass band used to play. It was held on our farm, on the field known as Penyrheol Ten Acres.

In the village, there was earlier a small shop at Village Farm, but it is the village shop-cum-post office opposite the Carne Arms which I remember. My cousin William Thomas, Moorshead, and I would sometimes go in before school and buy five Woodbines for 2d. These we would share, two and a half each, and smoke the half before school. On one occasion, Miss

Llysworney Show, August 1930

(L to R): Davy Jones, Rees Thomas, Dai Harris (blacksmith and clerk of the Show), Mr Grant, Morgan Thomas - Moorshead, Gil Board, Mrs Carne, Ernie Golden - Colwinston, Capt Carne, ? , Thomas Rogers Thomas

Grant was bending over me to check what I had written when she smelled the smoke on my breath, and she wrote to my father to let him know what was going on. However, my father was a heavy smoker himself, and so I don't think he said too much to us. My grandfather's reaction was worse, at least when we'd said in the shop 'Grandpa will pay' - and, of course, when checking the bill he found us out straight away, as he didn't smoke Woodbines.

As our school was a Church in Wales school, every Saint's Day we went to church. The parson was Dr Llewellyn, the vicar of Llysworney and

Llandow (the grandfather of Dr David Owen, MP). He was a lovely man, who had been blind since his boyhood, as a result of playing dog and catty, we were told. He used to come to school frequently, and found his way without difficulty, even though Llysworney school was not the easiest place to get to. We were always sent to assist him, but he was very independent and did not want help.

We played a lot of the usual games - spinning tops, hopscotch, and hoops. If we didn't have a metal hoop, we would sometimes use tyres. I remember on one occasion when I was using a tyre down the road, it ran away from me and landed with a thump in the door of the Carne Arms. Mrs Howell rushed out, not well pleased!

In 1934, they started laying the water mains from Llysworney past our farm. One day, on my way to Sunday school, I passed the compressor which was standing idle because it was the weekend. There were bigger boys playing around it, fiddling with the starting handle. On my return from Sunday school, there was nobody around the machine, so I gave it one idle turn of the starting handle - and it started! What was I to do? The machine was all locked up and so could not be stopped; I ran round it frantically, and then ran home, where the family were sitting around the table, having tea. I joined them, but from the house I could hear the noise of the machine, and so I left the table and ran off into the fields. Eventually I returned to hear my mother talking to PC Cosslett, who was 'winding her up' in terms of the potential dangers of starting up the machine. What annoyed my mother, however, was that the foreman of the water main gang, who lived in the village, had reported me - and yet a few weeks earlier he had come to my father for help in writing a letter! Even though all I got was a ticking off from the policeman, for many weeks I had to endure the calls of the men 'Come and help us start it, Alan' as I passed them on my way to school.

Another memory of Llysworney was of the small field we called Gypsy's Acre. On this piece of land belonging to my grandfather, behind the church - there are two or three houses built on it now - three of my uncles, all bachelors, lived in three caravans. One was a real gypsy caravan, all brass and glass, while the others were more utilitarian.

When my father died in 1938, my mother had Ty Bronudd built on the Nash corner, and we moved there. By then, I was a day boy at the Grammar School (I think I was the third boy from the village school to pass the eleven-plus examination), and travelled in by bus. When war broke out in 1939 I was still at school. For the first few months of the war Cowbridge was a garrison town. Large numbers of territorials were mobilised and were billeted in the town. Every available public building was commandeered: the Town Hall, the first floor of the cinema (which contained a large dance hall and sundry rooms, whilst the cinema continued to function below), and the Grammar School's new dining hall and gymnasium. The school buildings had only been opened the year before, providing day boys with proper dining facilities and a first class gym. As pupils we had been made to take care of the wood block floors (we had to change into gym shoes whenever we entered the building, be it for lunch or gym), and suddenly it was invaded by soldiers in army boots, and the polished surface rapidly became pock-marked with stud marks.

RAF Station St Athan was opened in 1938, so Cowbridge was used to the sight of airmen in blue uniform, the first airmen at St Athan wearing a type of breeches. (RAF Llandow was opened in about 1940.) The headquarters for the army, however, was the Duke of Wellington Inn, and the entrance was protected with a sand-bagged porch jutting out onto the pavement. The town echoed to the sound of troops marching about during the day, often singing marching songs, 'Roll out the Barrel' being a very popular one. The sound of bugle calls rang out, 'Reveille' in the morning and 'The Last Post' at night.

There were also soldiers stationed in small units in the countryside around the town, manning searchlights. I remember one of them who, not being used to the country, shot a cow which he heard moving behind a hedge.

In school, we carried on as normally as possible, but rugby fixtures were cancelled for the first term and we played the army in some soccer matches. The Bear Field (where the Leisure Centre is now) was at that time also one of the school's playing fields. While the army was in Cowbridge, this was used by the military, so we were allowed to use the town pitch in the Athletic Ground. The blackout was a problem in the evenings as all windows had to be covered with thick material to prevent the showing of any light. All street lights were extinguished and this again caused a problem at night, especially with the sand-bagged enclosures protruding onto the pavement. It gave one an uncomfortable experience to walk into a wall of sand bags.

The soldiers departed as quickly as they arrived and, by the end of the year, they had gone.

The Howells family of the Carne Arms, and friends

One of the wartime schemes that was encouraged was 'Digging for Victory', in which people were urged to grow as much vegetable produce as possible. The school responded to this: the produce was used in its own kitchens, thus saving money! Seniors were put to dig up all the ground around the gym and dining hall and plant cabbages and potatoes. The work was supervised by Mr Penny, the school gardener. The work was carried out in what would have been those school periods devoted to non-academic subjects such as woodwork.

After Dunkirk, the LDV (Local Defence Volunteers), the fore-runner of the Home Guard, was formed. It consisted mainly of elderly men and young boys. I joined straight away, when I was in school, and I always carried my arm band in my pocket. When an air raid warning went, all the pupils were supposed to take cover in safe rooms, which had been reinforced with timbers to give some protection. I used to slip out of school and report to our armoury, which at that time was in the Town Hall, collect a rifle and a bandolier of ammunition and, along with other members of the LDV, man the road blocks which were at the main entrances to the town.

The road blocks were on the Cardiff road at the railway bridge, on the Aberthin road near the High School, and up at the Darren. These road blocks were manned every night by a platoon of six to eight men. During an air raid warning, all vehicles and pedestrians were stopped and identity cards had to be produced. In the blackout it was quite a risky business stopping vehicles, especially on the Cardiff road as the vehicles were coming downhill, with very limited lights. They were stopped by the guard swinging a hurricane lamp. We would even inspect all the passengers in the buses. This proved to be very difficult with a rifle slung over one's shoulder. The barricades were constructed of all sorts of material, and the one on the Aberthin road included an old horse-drawn stage coach in which the guards often took shelter during poor weather. There were also posts at Penllyn and St Hilary.

The first bombs dropped in the Cowbridge area were on the Stalling Down. They came down at night and, because of the rocky surface of the ground, they made quite an impact and a number of houses suffered minor damage. The only other bombs dropped in Cowbridge were across the railway line behind the High School; these were fire bombs and did no damage as they landed in open ground.

Later on the guards were withdrawn from the road blocks and we billeted in the Town Hall. You can imagine the noise with about twenty to thirty men trying to sleep on the floor of the hall. During an air raid warning a patrol would be sent out. I think the reason was to watch out for paratroops. The Town Hall was a very busy place; as well as being the HQ of the Home Guard, as it was by then known, the Red Cross ambulance had a unit stationed in the Mayor's Parlour. The air raid wardens were in another room downstairs and of course the fire brigade with their engine was also in what is now the kitchen of the Lesser Hall. Bill Brown, who was a self-appointed sergeant major as well as being the caretaker to the Town Hall, was quite a character. He had all the bearing of a sergeant major, wore a fine waxed moustache and carried a cane under his arm. During the time the Home Guard was in the Town Hall, Bill Brown used to get up every morning and come up to dismiss the guard. He would be immaculately turned out, yet without his false teeth.

The next move for the Home Guard was up to a building where JB Builders Merchants now have their office. The nightly guard was then down to a unit of about six men and a sergeant. These evening guard duties always finished at five o'clock in the morning.

Another character was the CO, Reg Williams the chemist. He was a captain, and Captain Mainwaring of Dad's Army was the personification of Reg. He was very enthusiastic and devoted a great deal of time to the Home Guard. Whenever the air raid warning went, Captain Williams could be seen emerging from the chemist's shop, strapping on a huge revolver around his waist.

We were expected to attend a parade one evening a week, and on Sunday mornings. We drilled, learned about weapons, went on exercises and all the other things necessary to train us for fighting the Germans in the event of an invasion. We practised firing our weapons down at the army range at Porthcawl and also at the old butts near the river at Llandough Mill. We were quite well equipped - not as it was usually depicted with pikes and poles. I had my own rifle from very early on and before I left to join the RAF (I was a sergeant by then) I had a Sten sub-machine gun.

The ATC unit in school under the command of Mr 'Taffy' Hughes was not formed until after I left; they apparently had a miniature rifle range in the roof of the Old Hall, but that is another story.

Cowbridge Record Society

This society was set up to collect, record, preserve and publish information relating to the history of Cowbridge and district.

Earlier publications were:

Cowbridge Buildings and People	(ISBN 0 9537029 0 1)
At Cowbridge Grammar School 1949–1966	(ISBN 0 9537029 1 X)
Llanblethian Buildings and People	(ISBN 0 9537029 2 8)

Detailed references to the sources used in the 'Buildings and People' books are also available–the Cowbridge volume, which has been deposited in selected libraries and research centres in Wales, is now being revised.

Membership of the society costs £3 a year, and gives discounts on publications, an occasional newsletter, and the satisfaction of knowing that members are helping to preserve some of the heritage of the area.

To join the society, please contact the treasurer,

DK Jones,
48 Eastgate,
Cowbridge,
CF71 7AB